THE ORDEAL
OF THE
HERMITAGE

THE ORDEAL OF THE HERMITAGE

THE SIEGE OF LENINGRAD· 1941 - 1944

Text by Sergei Varshavsky and Boris Rest

AURORA ART PUBLISHERS, LENINGRAD·
HARRY N. ABRAMS, INC., PUBLISHERS, NEW YORK

TRANSLATED FROM THE RUSSIAN BY ARTHUR SHKAROVSKY-RAFFÉ
LAYOUT BY LIUBOV RAKHMILEVICH
COLOR PHOTOGRAPHS BY VICTOR SAVIK AND LEONID BOGDANOV

Library of Congress Catalog Card Number: 85-6137
ISBN 0-8109-1406-9

Created by Aurora Art Publishers, Leningrad, for joint publication
of Aurora and Harry N. Abrams, Inc., New York

Printed and bound in Finland

Four decades separate us from the days with which the present volume is concerned, a span of time that allows us to review the past and bring to light the most important aspects of life in Leningrad during the siege. Tales of those days usually feature emotional accounts dealing with human sufferings and death, accounts that can never be forgotten, of course, and will remain as a dire indictment of war in the memory of future generations. In the life of besieged Leningrad a notable peculiarity manifested itself: an uncommon spiritual strength, a power of endurance, tenacity and chivalry of the thousands of men and women who rose to the defence of their city.

One of the pages of the city's heroic chronical of those days was the battle to save the art treasures created over the millennia by the genius of humanity, now in the custody of the Hermitage Museum.

The "greatest conquerors" of all time and all nations applied themselves to the task of destroying everything created by the world's renowned craftsmen.

The full significance of Leningrad's defence and final victory will be understood only if we weigh the meaning of the following facts: for 900 days and nights the magnificent city built by celebrated architects and glorified by renowned poets was bombed and shelled. According to a special commission, damage to the city's monuments amounted to two billion roubles. After the war, restoration workers aided by the men and women of Leningrad, by the entire nation, as a matter of fact, scored a new achievement by rebuilding what had been destroyed, even if not entirely, for many monuments had been damaged beyond repair.

Looking back on the arduous road we travelled during the war years, and honouring the memory of those who died defending our city, we can be satisfied that our work, carried on in unbelievably difficult conditions, had not been in vain: the collections of the Hermitage have been preserved, its buildings and interiors restored and its exhibitions enlarged.

The book in your hands acquaints you convincingly with the heroic efforts of the Hermitage staff during the war, and with the priceless treasures which were saved from destruction and increased during the years devoted to the restoration of the museum and the years of peace that followed.

BORIS PIOTROVSKY,
Director of the State Hermitage

ACKNOWLEDGEMENTS

The Publishers are grateful to the following art scholars working under Boris Piotrovsky, Director of the State Hermitage, who contributed to the present volume:

Galina Komelova, Tamara Kudriavtseva, Maria Malchenko, Vladimir Matveyev, and Karina Orlova of the Russian Department;
Sergei Androsov, Nina Biriukova, Anna Voronikhina, Yulia Kagan, Nina Kosareva, Yuri Kuznetsov, Zavel Lerman, Marina Lopato, Olga Mikhailova, Tamara Rappe, Yuri Rusakov, Roda Soloveychik, Vladimir Chernyshov, Yuri Yefimov, Yuri Miller, and Alexei Shevchenko of the Western European Department;
Tatyana Arapova, Vera Zalesskaya, Anatoly Ivanov, Natalia Landa, and Vladimir Lukonin of the Oriental Department;
Nina Kunina, Irina Saverkina, Elena Khodza of the Department of Classical Antiquity;
Maria Zavitukhina of the Department of Primitive Culture;
Ivan Spassky and Evgeniya Shchukina of the Department of Numismatics.

The Publishers are also grateful to the workers of the Hermitage Archives Galina Kachalina and Valentina Marishkina.

For permission to publish documentary materials in this volume acknowledgement is made to the staff of the Hermitage Archives, Archives of Photographs of the USSR Academy of Arts (photographs by S. Gasilov) and the Museum of the History of Leningrad.

In the autumn of 1945 the ancient German town of Nuremberg became the scene of an unprecedented trial in the history of Justice. The International Military Tribunal comprising lawyers of the Soviet Union, Britain, the USA and France tried major Nazi war criminals accused of crimes against peace and humanity.

The trial lasted for ten months and eleven days. In February 1946, after the International Tribunal had presided for three months, the judges proceeded to examine that point in the indictment that was concerned with the destruction and plunder of cultural treasures. The Soviet prosecution took the floor to present the evidence. Day after day more and more irrefutable proof was adduced. Time and again the documentary films, demonstrating the wretched and ruined cultural monuments that the Nazi occupying forces had left behind, were shown. Then came the moment when one of the Soviet prosecutors requested permission from the presiding judge to question a witness, Academician Iosif Orbeli, who had flown to Nuremberg to bear witness as to the destruction of Leningrad's cultural and art monuments.

A slightly stooped gentleman of medium height entered the court-room and took his place at the witness-box ("with hair like King Lear's and a majestically flowing beard, a most impressive personality," the newsman would describe him later). An Orientalist of international repute, well-known to his fellow-countrymen present in the court-room, Orbeli was a name that meant nothing to the tourists cramming the visitors' gallery and even to most of the correspondents representing the world press. But they learned that the imposing elderly gentleman, now standing at the witness-box, had come from the city which had withstood an unprecedented 900-day siege of unparalleled harshness and cruelty, and the silence slightly disturbed by the appearance of the witness again fell on the court-room.

"Would you please state your present office," the Soviet prosecution addressed Academician Iosif Orbeli.

"I am Director of the State Hermitage."

The hall buzzed. Everyone had heard of this world-famous Leningrad museum.

*　　*　　*

The Hermitage... What an odd name for a museum of stupendous scope, renowned throughout the world not only for its vast collections of rarities and treasures but also for the immense crowds thronging its halls! Fancy a hermitage, which would seem to imply a place of solitary isolation for a lonely recluse, with an annual attendance of some three and a half million!

To understand why one of the world's most visited museums bears this strange name, allow us to take you, dear reader, on a brief armchair excursion into Russia's past. Imagine yourself in the St. Petersburg of the 1740s, only a few decades after Russia's Emperor, Peter the Great, had founded his new city at the mouth of the Neva River, to "open a window on Europe," as the great Russian poet Alexander Pushkin said in one of his poems, and had made it the capital of his vast domain.

The year is 1744 and on the Russian throne now is Peter's daughter Elizabeth.

When in 1744 Sophia Augusta Frederika (the future Empress Catherine II), daughter of the Prince of Anhalt-Zerbst, arrived in St. Petersburg from Pomerania to marry the Grand Duke Peter, heir to the imperial throne of Russia, she was amazed at the luxury of the Russian court. Though Elizabeth considered her winter residence dilapidated and was already thinking of building a new palace on the Neva's banks, the princess gazed wonderstruck at the exquisitely furnished apartments. She was equally impressed by the magnificent Throne Hall and a secluded nook, which the Empress had arranged for more intimate receptions much in the manner of the French kings at Versailles, and which was facetiously called the "hermitage."

It took the celebrated Russian architect Bartolommeo Francesco Rastrelli ten years to erect the new palace that the Empress so ardently desired but in which she was not fated to live: she died in 1761, a few weeks before its completion, and it remained for the new Emperor, who ascended the throne under the name of Peter III, to make it his imperial residence. Three months later his wife, Catherine II, however, deposed him to become the despotic ruler of Russia's far-flung territories and full mistress of the Winter Palace. She also arranged a hermitage for herself in this newly built edifice. However, this worldly-wise, thirty-three-year-old Empress, skilled not only in amorous, but also in political intrigue, resolved that even in her private life she would serve her realm. As soon as she ascended the throne she instructed her envoys to foreign lands to keep close watch on every auction and sale, so as not to overlook a single painting or statue worthy of adorning "Her Imperial Majesty's Hermitage." Though her treasury was by no means bursting at the seams, she was unsparing of money to purchase works of art and precious baubles, all to create the reputation of an enlightened monarch and a grand patron of the arts, and to impress upon the flabbergasted kings, bankers and philosophers of Europe that her domains were flourishing and that beggarly, serf-burdened Russia was thriving under her reign.

However, the Hermitage is regarded as having started out as a museum in 1764. By this year a great number of fine works of art had been collected in the rooms in the Winter Palace and the Empress, in order to augment her hermitage, entrusted her architect, Vallin de La Mothe, with the task of building a special pavilion adjacent to the Winter Palace and looking out on the Neva River. But, when after the passage of several years, these premises were also found inadequate, the architect Yuri Velten was ordered to construct one more three-storey building, in order to bring the suite of palace rooms up to the Winter Canal, a narrow waterway linking the Neva with the Moika River. Subsequently, the architect Giacomo Quarenghi built on the other side of the Winter Canal, where Peter the Great had once had his residence, the Hermitage Theatre "for the private use of Her Imperial Majesty," and connected the Hermitage proper with it by means of a small glassed-in bridge spanning the canal.

Today, de La Mothe's pavilion is known as the Small Hermitage, and Velten's building as the Old Hermitage.

Meanwhile, Catherine's agents paid enormous sums of money for individual paintings and entire collections. Strings of carts loaded high with precious works of art for "Her Imperial Majesty's Hermitage" came to Russia from various countries of Europe and many a sailing ship dropped anchor off the Neva's quays to discharge priceless Titians, Murillos, Rubenses, Van Dycks, Rembrandts and Poussins. Bragging of the untold gems in her possession that filled her place of retreat, the Empress wrote to a correspondent in Paris: "Only the mice and I admire all this..."

"Her Imperial Majesty's Hermitage is thus named from its designation to serve for the private amusements and exercises of Catherine the Second,"

1

Several rooms in the new palace built to the design of Bartolommeo Francesco Rastrelli as a winter residence for Russian tsars were allotted by Catherine II for her "hermitage."

View of the Winter Palace
Drawing by Mikhail Makhayev. 1750s

states the first-ever account of Catherine's Hermitage made during her life-time. But even after her death, in the reign of Alexander I, when the Hermitage was first referred to as a museum, only a few select people "of certified worth" were admitted, with a flunkey strictly ordered to attach himself to each such visitor. Several pertinent documents of the time assiduously note that "the Hermitage is not a public museum but a continuation of the Imperial Palace."

In the mid-nineteenth century a new building (on the Palace Square side) designed as a continuation of the Winter Palace was completed and called the New Hermitage. It was to the New Hermitage, specially designated to house the museum collections and having a picture gallery with skylights, spacious exhibition halls and granite atlantes at the entrance, that the innumerable collections of the Hermitage were moved. The Great Hermitage was renamed the Old Hermitage and the Small Hermitage was adapted to other requirements.

"The fortunate thought of converting this 'hermitage' into a proper, well-established museum occurred to the Emperor Nicholas I," the then official history of the Imperial Hermitage notes. This seems blasphemous. Imagine a cruel despot, a hangman of poet and artist and a persecutor of enlightened thought, suddenly organizing a public art museum that amazed contemporaries and rightly occupied a place of honour among the world's top museums. By modernizing the Hermitage this

4

View of the Hermitage Theatre from the Neva
Sepia by Pietro Gonzaga. 1790s

5

View of the New Hermitage from the south-east
Watercolour by Vasily Sadovnikov. 1851

2

2

View of Palace
Square and the Winter
Palace from Nevsky
Prospekt
Engraving by
Mathias Gabriel Lori
the Younger after
Benjamin
Paterssen's original.
1804

3

View of the Palace
Embankment
from the Peter
and Paul Fortress
Painting by
Fiodor Alexeyev.
Early 19th century

6

7

8

9

10

11

12

13

14

6

The Jordan Staircase of the Winter Palace
Watercolour by Konstantin Ukhtomsky

7

The Pompeii Dining-room in the Winter Palace
Watercolour by Konstantin Ukhtomsky. 1874

8

The Concert Hall in the Winter Palace
Watercolour by Konstantin Ukhtomsky

9

The Malachite Room in the Winter Palace
Watercolour by Konstantin Ukhtomsky. 1865

10

The Armorial Hall in the Winter Palace
Watercolour by Edward Hau. 1863

11

The Pavilion Hall in the Small Hermitage
Watercolour by Edward Hau. 1864

12

The Room of Italian Painting
(The Greater Skylighted Room) in the New Hermitage
Watercolour by Edward Hau. 1853

13

The Tent Hall in the New Hermitage
Watercolour by Ludwig Premazzi. 1858

14

Part of the Eastern Gallery in the Small Hermitage
Watercolour by Konstantin Ukhtomsky. 1860

15

15

Gallery of the History of Antique Painting
Watercolour by Edward Hau. 1859

16

The Main Staircase and Lobby in the New Hermitage
Watercolour by Konstantin Ukhtomsky. 1853

17

Boudoir in the Winter Palace
Watercolour by Edward Hau. 1861

17

18

16

19

21

20

18

Drawing-room in the Winter Palace
Watercolour by Edward Hau. 1868

19

The Room of Greek and Etruscan Vases
(The Hall of Twenty Columns) in the New Hermitage
Watercolour by Konstantin Ukhtomsky

20

The Room of the Antiquities from the Cimmerian Bosporus
Watercolour by Konstantin Ukhtomsky

21

Voltaire's Library in the New Hermitage
Watercolour by Konstantin Ukhtomsky. 1859

22

Sculpture Room in the New Hermitage
Watercolour by Konstantin Ukhtomsky. 1854

22

harsh monarch merely sought to re-adapt the lessons of his regal grandmother — this magnificent "Imperial Museum" was to entrench in the minds of the loyalist Russian and sceptical foreigner the staunch conviction that even then, despite the tide of revolution sweeping Europe, Russia continued to flourish under the reign of a powerful and confident autocrat.

Drawing up his plans for the New Hermitage, the Munich architect Leo von Klenze proceeded from the basic point made by the commissioner that the museum should be a part of the imperial residence. Such was the guiding rule, too, of the court officials in charge of the museum: admission to the museum was strictly limited. Only towards the turn of the twentieth century did the Chancellery of

24

The bronze plaque on the palace façade tells about
the historic storming of the Winter Palace on October 25
(November 7, N.S.), 1917

Hermitage Museum. Long before the war against Nazi Germany, the Hermitage already had in its inventory a total of 1,600,000 items. Another quarter-million works of art were added during the few years preceding the war. Today the Hermitage boasts a collection of two and a half million items.

However, back to Nuremberg where the International Military Tribunal was trying major Nazi war criminals. In the witness-box is Iosif Orbeli, Academician and Director of the Hermitage Museum.

"I, Iosif Orbeli, a citizen of the Soviet Union," he declares, "subpoenaed as a witness, hereby swear before this High Court to tell the truth and nothing but the truth about everything I know as concerns this case."

23

*For one hundred and fifty years the Hermitage buildings
were a continuation of the Winter Palace. In 1917
the October Revolution, which shifted all social accents
in Russia, made the former royal residence a continuation
of the State Hermitage.*

Panoramic view of the Hermitage buildings from the Neva

the Imperial Court, taking extreme precautions, extend admission to the lower orders. Even so, right up to 1917, the Hermitage administration considered itself bound by the statement made in the catalogue issued upon the opening of the New Hermitage that "The Hermitage Palace is no more than a continuation of the Winter Palace."

It was only after the October Revolution, which shifted all social accents in Russia, that the Winter Palace became an integral part of the Hermitage Museum. The unprecedented augmentation of the Hermitage collections necessitated that not only the Winter Palace, the former royal residence, but also the Old Hermitage and the Small Hermitage should be incorporated within the

The testimony that Academician Orbeli presented at the Nuremberg trial — together with other much authenticated evidence, such as official references, records, notes, memoires, photographs and, finally, the drawings and sketches made by artists in the besieged Leningrad — has provided the documentary background for the following narrative about the Hermitage's wartime vicissitudes and of how this world-famous museum was saved for humanity.

★　　★　　★

The summer months always show peak attendance at the Hermitage and of all the days in the week Sunday is naturally the top favourite for visiting a museum.

It was a summer Sunday, that memorable Sunday of June 22, 1941. The Government announcement of Nazi Germany's perfidious attack on the USSR, of war, which had broken out at dawn, came only at noon, when it grew absolutely clear at the Kremlin that no diplomatic venture could stop the enemy invasion. Up to that fateful noon the people of Leningrad went about their usual Sunday pursuits. At 11 o'clock in the morning the Hermitage opened its doors and the crowds moved in to fill its rooms and halls. Unmindful of other cares and concerns, the thousands paused to gaze enraptured at the Rembrandts and the Raphaels or admire the antiques in the ground-floor rooms. Some sought out the artifacts recovered from Khara-Khoto, others wished to see the Renoirs and the Degases, others were interested in the Egyptian mummies or wanted to see the marble sculpture of Voltaire. It was getting near midday, but nobody at the Hermitage, be it a visitor, a guide, a curator or an attendant knew that the Nazi barbarians had crashed through the country's borders, that fierce fighting had been going on for several hours already and that for their city of Leningrad the sands of peace had run out.

Exactly at midday a gun fired and in the windows facing the Neva the panes tinkled. This was a gun mounted on the Peter and Paul Fortress on the other side of the river, a very peaceful gun which gave its blank shot daily to announce midday. But as the gun fired its time signal there came from the radios in the Hermitage's back rooms that fateful announcement of war. "German forces," it said, "have attacked our country, our frontiers in many sectors and have bombed our cities and towns from the air..."

Soon the halls became absolutely deserted. The absence of a single soul, so amazing for the Hermitage's rush hours, so incredible in the midst of a summer Sunday, brought home more forcefully perhaps than anything else that henceforth nothing here would be the same again.

Towards evening the museum staff was warned that the evacuation of the Hermitage's treasures would commence very shortly, if not on the morrow, then on the day after. The government announcement had mentioned air-raids from nearby Finland and hence any delay with evacuation would be most hazardous. A network of barrage balloons had gone up and all of the Hermitage staff listed in the air-raid warden roster were henceforth to stay in the museum round the clock.

At a quarter to two in the early hours of the morning of June 23, the air-raid sirens blasted off and an excited voice announced an air alert over the radio. The air-raid wardens at once rushed to their posts in the halls, on the rooftops and by the doors and gates. The skies, the usual white-night June skies, stretched above the hushed city, above the Neva and the wide square in front of the Winter Palace. They were as serene and cloudless as they had been each night before.

The air-raid wardens peered into the skies overhead. The buildings seemed to tower up in full stature as if ready to brave the deadly enemy bombardment. Meanwhile about forty of the Old Masters, the most precious masterpieces, had been taken down from the Picture Gallery and stowed away beneath the arched vaults of the Hermitage's most reliable shelter. In the same manner as during the future sleepless nights of air attacks, Leningrad's children, womenfolk and senior citizens would huddle for safety in the many air-raid shelters, so now several sentimentally touching Italian ladies with babes in arms, in the company of sad old men and women from the distant Amsterdam of Rembrandt, spent the first war night in the darkness of the Gold Room, the Museum's Special Vault.

Not a single enemy aircraft got through that night. Which did not mean, though, that the Nazi air force would desist from attempts to break through into Leningrad's skies and rain bombs down upon the vast city. The Hermitage staff persistently telephoned the Committee for Art Affairs in Moscow appealing for help. Evacuation of the Hermitage treasures could not be delayed.

25
The Main Staircase
in the Winter Palace
Designed
by Bartolommeo
Francesco Rastrelli,
1753–59; rebuilt
by Vasily Stasov,
1837–39

26
The Field Marshal Hall in the Winter Palace
Designed by Auguste Montferrand, 1833;
rebuilt by Vasily Stasov, 1837–38

The Hermitage's entire staff, the keepers, the curators, the researchers, the librarians, the restorers, the watchmen, the attendants and the cleaners, responded at once to the call from Moscow to prepare immediately for evacuation. Heaven knows from whence came the hundreds of crates of varying sizes and dimensions already mysteriously numbered and lettered, or from whence came the huge rolls of packing paper, some waxed and glossy, some rough and hard-wearing, some tissue-soft, the bales of compressed shavings, the mountains of cotton wool, the sacks of crumbled cork, and the mile-long lengths of oil-cloth! All this seemed to descend like manna from heaven as if by the wave of a magic wand.

It must be noted, though, that when the Nazi jackboots first marched down the roads of Europe and not only people living beyond the Pyrenees learned to identify the roar of Nazi aircraft, the Hermitage's administrators had devised detailed evacuation plans, should the fires of war that Hitler had lit scorch Soviet borders. Storehouses were filled with packaging, and the necessary containers for the Hermitage treasures had lain for years gathering dust — in much the same manner as army trenchcoats and highboots are stowed away as reserves. And so, storehouse doors were unsealed and flung open and the empty crates were trundled up to the halls and galleries.

There, a number of massive crates, made of thick, well-shaved pine-wood planks, were deposited on the floor of the Rembrandt Room. Flora, her head crowned with a wreath of wild flowers, Danaë, half-rising from her couch, the scholar of Amsterdam, his eyes turned away from the book before him, all stared at the packaging that awaited them. Meanwhile *The Holy Family*, already taken down from the wall and removed from its carved gilt frame, had been laid to rest at the bottom of a flat casing and fixed tight by means of padded wedges.

The fate of the Old Masters largely depended on how well they would now be handled and packed; no wonder that the techniques employed were time and again noted by all chronicles of the Hermitage's history:

"Pictures of small and medium format were stacked away in crates outfitted with cloth-padded parallel dividers, in between which they neatly fitted and were held in place by wooden blocks. One such crate could hold between twenty and sixty paintings. Larger pictures were removed from their stretchers and rolled over rollers, with each roller taking from ten to fifteen canvases with layers of tissue paper between them. After that the rollers were placed in oil-cloth casings, deposited in long, flat boxes and lashed tight."

In the Rembrandt Room *David and Uriah*, *Flora*, *Danaë*, *The Portrait of a Scholar* and *The Parable of the Labourers in the Vineyard* had been removed from the walls and were in process of being packed; elsewhere Rubens's *Bacchus* and *Portrait of a Lady-in-Waiting*, Titian's *Danaë* and *St Mary Magdalene in Penitence*, Giorgione's *Judith*, El Greco's *St Peter and St Paul*, Murillo's *Boy with a Dog*, Van Dyck's *Self-portrait*, Poussin's *Landscape with Polythemus*, Watteau's *Capricious Girl*, the paintings of Velázquez, Delacroix, Hals, David, Caravaggio, Gainsborough, Tiepolo and Cézanne, in short, thousands of canvases of diverse epochs and schools were taken down off the walls and removed from their frames. The paintings, which for years had hung in strictly regimented order, in full accordance with their chronology and provenance, were now jumbled in

27
The Malachite Room in the Winter Palace
Designed by Alexander Briullov. 1838–39

28
The Private Dining-room in the Winter Palace
Designed by Alexander Krasovsky. 1894

confusion, haphazardly waiting to be duly packed and posted, much like a motley, multi-lingual crowd of passengers may patiently, or perhaps not so patiently, wait at the different railway stations for a transcontinental express. Not to say that there was no pattern to this seeming disarray; everything went according to the pre-arranged scheme of things whereby the corresponding number of accurately listed and titled pictures of identical size were to be put in their respective crates as designated by the black-stencilled numbers and letters carried on their sides. In short, each crate was intended for a definite list of paintings and each painting had its definite place in the evacuation pattern.

However, there were thousands upon thousands of paintings to be handled. No matter how many willing and capable hands the Hermitage staff had, they were not enough to crate the smaller pieces and gingerly remove from their frames and wrap around the rollers the hundreds of larger masterpieces, all within an impossible timetable.

In this hour of need Leningrad's artistic community volunteered to help. Whether elderly well-established artists of renown, 'the newer generation of Soviet times, or the dedicated students of the Academy of Arts, they approached the Hermitage paintings as old friends and revered companions. Indeed, how many an hour had been spent in blissful admiration before the Old Masters, experiencing the sense of communion felt by all true artists ever since the days of the famous Russian painters Venetsianov (1780–1847) and Fedotov (1815–1852) and their colleagues. Indeed in the 1930s, in the same manner as a hundred years earlier, aspiring youthful painters, garbed in paint-besmeared smocks, their hearts palpitating with reverent awe, would enter the sunlit halls and galleries, and set up the tripods of portable easels, to learn the secrets of the craft, the skill of the brushwork, the magic of the chiaroscuro.

However, paradoxically enough, only now in these hours of confusion, amidst the yawning crates and the rolls of packing paper, were they able for the first time to see the Old Masters in all their pristine freshness, without the artful gilded carving of Baroque frames, in the noble nakedness of a newly born work of art, as they had appeared two, three or, perchance, a full five hundred years ago to the artists of Florence, Amsterdam or Paris, who, having applied the last stroke, stepped back in their studios and ateliers to view their creations.

As in the hour of their birth, as during the first few days of their centuries-long lives, the canvases stood there, frameless, ranged along the walls and in between the windows, trustingly surrendering themselves to the confident hands of Leningrad artists, who radiated the so familiar smells of pigment, oil and varnish.

The only picture to have a crate all its own was *The Return of the Prodigal Son*, perhaps the greatest creation of the already partly blind Rembrandt. It was a grand masterpiece that drew art-lovers — and does to this day — to the Hermitage from all over the world. Nobody would have ever dared to remove this enormous canvas (262 cm high and 205 cm wide, or a total of 5.37 square metres) from its frame and roll it round a roller as was done with other large paintings. Moreover, the three-centimetre-thick casing, which had been specially prepared for *The Return of the Prodigal Son*, only added to the dimensions; and though the size had been known beforehand, none could rid themselves of the fear that it might not squeeze through the wide doors of a goods car.

Among the works of art thus packed for speedy evacuation were pastels, some on gritty paper, others on parchment and still others on canvas, velvety and soft, and tender and as sensitive as hothouse flowers; indeed, pastels are customarily never unsealed from their glass casings, as the slightest perturbation causes the powder to fall off and even the slightest contact with the glass framing will cause them to smudge. For that reason, the pastels were left in their glass frames; the glass was reinforced by glueing paper on it; each piece was inserted in a sheath of plywood and secured within the box, which itself was lined with oilcloth from within and without. Drawings and engravings filled other boxes into which also went cardboard boxes holding miniatures lovingly wrapped in several layers of tissue paper.

From the upstairs halls and rooms the crates and boxes were carried down and readied for loading. Meanwhile more crates and coffers were trundled into the Hermitage's Special Vault, the Gold Room, a place without windows and with steel-faced doors, the spot where the da Vincis and Raphaels,

29

The Greater
Skylighted Room
in the New Hermitage
Built by
Vasily Stasov
and Nikolai Yefimov
after Leo von
Klenze's design.
1842–51

30

The Snyders Room
in the New Hermitage
Built by
Vasily Stasov
and Nikolai Yefimov
after Leo von
Klenze's design.
1842–51

31

The Pavilion Hall in
the Small Hermitage
Designed by Andrei
Stakenschneider.
1850–58

Rembrandts and Rubenses had spent the first night of the war. In this strongroom electric lamps burn day and night and in their bleak glow, all that is known under its generic title of Scythian Gold sparkles and gleams. Peter the Great's celebrated Siberian Collection has been augmented by gold artifacts recovered from Scythian royal burials in Southern Russia and today the Hermitage collection of Scythian art is the world's richest, second to none.

Displayed in other glass cases nearby are gold objects from Ancient Greece. Though the statue of Pallas Athena, wrought by Phidias, is irrevocably lost, the face of the Greek goddess, or rather its faithful representation, recreated in miniature by an anonymous goldsmith of Ancient Greece, continues to look out at us from the gold pendants, which some twenty-five centuries ago chanced to find their way into the cypress-wood coffin unearthed in the Kul-Oba tumulus. Truth to tell, many a majestic representation of ancient monumental statuary that has been forever lost to humanity is indebted for its immortal fame to the miniatures produced by the keen-eyed goldsmiths of Ancient Greece, to those elegant, refined items of Hellenistic jewellery of which the Hermitage boasts a priceless collection.

The Gold Room's cold electric incandescence is reflected in scintillating rainbow profusion by the clusters of diamonds adorning jewellery of the seventeenth, eighteenth and nineteenth centuries that seem strewn in veritable galactic formation on the dark velvet show cases, again in the Special Vault — which is actually a chain of rooms. "That gallery of precious gems which is now known as the Special Vault," Academician Alexander Fersman, that poet of mineralogy, wrote, "boasts the fullest

33

32,33

The White Hall in the Winter Palace
Designed by Alexander Briullov. 1837–39

34

Western Gallery in the Small Hermitage
Designed by Vasily Stasov. 1840–41

35

The Leonardo da Vinci Room
Designed by Andrei Stakenschneider. 1851–54

picture of the art of the jeweller, one of the loveliest of the creative arts. The decoration of all these baubles, fans, snuff-boxes, toilet cases, watches, jewellery caskets, cane-heads, signet rings, finger rings, etc., manifest so much aesthetic taste, so great an understanding of the ornamental aspects of gem and stone, so masterly a compositional arrangement and such virtuoso technique, that admiring all these items one perforce acknowledges their unpretentious and now-forgotten makers as worthy confreres of the great masters whose creations currently hang on the nearby walls of the Hermitage's Picture Gallery."

The Hermitage staff was given but six days and six nights to pack all the treasures confined in the Special Vault, and all the time, all six days and nights, the lights burned unceasingly in the strong-rooms of the Special Vault. The tissue paper rustled as carefully wrapped within it were the Scythian gold objects, the artful handiwork of the jewellers of Ancient Greece and the clusters of diamonds and gems. Gone now were the gleam and the sparkle, the glitter and the coruscating iridescence.

A number of researchers from the Hermitage's other sections and departments were helping the small team of the Special Vault staff. And it should necessarily be noted, indeed stressed, that not once did the several young women who had come down to help and who spent all six days and nights in the glow of electric lights behind the steel-faced doors allow themselves to let an admiring glance rest on these adornments with which women have bedecked themselves, have flaunted and paraded, since time immemorial. It was simply that these young women, wrapping and stowing away the baubles, had not a minute to spare to marvel at the pendants and armlets of the fashionable ladies of Athens, or to enjoy the beauty of the bracelets and finger rings of those unexcelled Russian belles, the two empresses, Elizabeth, daughter of Peter the Great, and Catherine the Great herself. They had not a second to try on one or another ring with a green- or yellow-tinted solitaire, a rare agate or unique ruby setting, an emerald or cat's eye, for though it took but a few seconds to wrap each ring in tissue paper, there were more than ten thousand pieces to be packed. With nimble fingers, they wrapped one item after another, embedded each piece in cotton wool and pads of shavings, deposited them in boxes, large and small, and laid these boxes in the shavings filling the iron-bound coffers. And so, on it went.

Another load of crates and boxes was dragged into the Hall of Twelve Columns, then known as the Coin Room, and hoisted up the wrought-iron staircase into a tall colonnaded open gallery. Helping the numismatists here were a group of Hermitage guides. This again comprised one of the paradoxes that the outbreak of the war had brought in its train, as Hermitage guides, conducting thousands of tours along the traditional routes, had never entered this numismatic sanctum before. Now they were there, and there they remained for the next six days and nights.

Under the tsars the Hermitage's numismatic collection, which started out with the coins that Peter the Great had acquired for his *Kunstkammer* (Cabinet of Curios), was augmented by the purchase of many world-famous collections, amassed at various times by both Russian and foreigner, and also by the rare specimens unearthed by industrious archaeologists and lucky treasure-hunters. Even prior to the October Revolution, it was rated a veritable treasure trove; meanwhile by the time the war broke out in 1941 it boasted some three hundred thousand coins, exclusive of duplicates.

All these treasures were laid out on special cloth-lined trays that were contained in a varied assortment of cabinets, each for coins of the same time and place. As each tray was taken out, the Keeper of the Numismatic Collection ticked off the inventory number on the evacuation list. Meanwhile, his helpers coiled tissue paper into long twists to separate from one another each row of gold, silver, bronze or copper circlets with all their sundry stamps and dies; now and again these were tiny bits of metal which had once served as a medium of exchange and which were now priceless relics of bygone empires and cultures. Next each tray had to be wrapped in cotton wool and encased in an envelope of stiff paper. The numismatists and their assistants had no more than six days and six nights to pack carefully hundreds of thousands of coins, mute witnesses of bygone millennia. Within this deadline they likewise had to complete the packaging of other treasures of the Numismatic Department: the collections of medals and orders and awards for merit.

TODAY AT FOUR O'CLOCK IN THE MORNING,

WITHOUT PRESENTING ANY CLAIMS

TO THE SOVIET GOVERNMENT

AND WITHOUT ANY DECLARATION OF WAR,

GERMAN TROOPS ATTACKED OUR COUNTRY,

ATTACKED OUR BORDERS AT MANY POINTS

AND BOMBED FROM THEIR AIRPLANES OUR CITIES...

From the statement of the Soviet Government
on the perfidious attack of Nazi Germany
June 22, 1941

Every conceivable misfortune and calamity that the historians of old had chronicled in accounts of famous sieges of impregnable fortresses and citadels starved into surrender and then laid waste by fire and sword, every conceivable instrument and weapon of destruction and death that could be culled from the darkness of history and that were multiplied by such sophisticated and supermodern means of annihilation as long-range artillery and bomber aircraft, in short, everything conceivable and inconceivable was employed by the Nazis to batter down the great Russian city. However, Leningrad staunchly defied the enemy, its gallant defenders displaying unexampled miracles of heroism.

37 Leningraders are listening to the announcement of the Nazi attack on the Soviet Union

38   Soviet patrolling aircraft over Leningrad

39   Military seamen patrolling the Neva Embankment
Posters read: "The enemies are at the gates of Leningrad! We will
do our duty and use all our strength to defend our native city!"

40 Barrage balloons in Nevsky Prospekt

41 Anti-aircraft battery on Vasilyevsky Island, opposite the Winter Palace

42

44

43

45

46

42–46 The winter of 1941–42
in the besieged Leningrad

ГРАЖДАНЕ!
ПРИ АРТОБСТРЕЛЕ
ЭТА СТОРОНА УЛИЦЫ
НАИБОЛЕЕ ОПАСНА

47 "Citizens! During the artillery shelling this side
of the street is especially dangerous"

51 The Great Palace in Peterhof

50 The Catherine Palace in Pushkin

52 The Palace in Pavlovsk

53 Monplaisir
in Peterhof

54

54 The New Hermitage

55 *The walls
of the Hermitage
are scarred
by shell- and
bomb-splinters;
the windows
are covered
with plywood.*
The Winter Palace

The days were long and hot and they worked with the windows flung wide open. Outside, the pigeons and sparrows that had nested in the carved eaves billed and cooed. The twitter of the birds and the ear-splitting roar of the aircraft barraging the city, the peaceful voices of yesterday and the war sounds of today, burst in through the open windows to dissolve into the continuous monotone of packaging. The thunder of war rolled as yet still far from Leningrad, being faintly echoed by the incessant hammering as the crates and boxes were nailed up and made ready for removal. The acrid smoke of the fires of war enveloped towns and villages hundreds of kilometres away and the smell of gunpowder was remote indeed; all that could be smelled of war thus far at the Hermitage were the mothballs sprinkled on the Isfahan and Kashgar rugs and carpets and the kerosene sprayed on the paper used to line the long Gobelin tapestries prior to their being rolled over the huge rollers that had been prepared specially for them.

The war was in its sixth day. Many of the Hermitage staff had already gone out to the fighting fronts to serve with the armies in the field. But at the Hermitage itself, the packaging continued without cease. Before the war the rooms and halls had no electric lighting, except for the security lights. However, thanks to Leningrad's white nights, work went on uninterruptedly except when there was an air-raid alert. There was more than enough to occupy each and every pair of hands, whether of eminent scholars, or of the charladies, of the guides and the carpenters, and the Hermitage "grannies," as the hall attendants were affectionately called, because they really were all elderly ladies. All pitched in, but still there were not enough pairs of hands to go round.

Experienced packers from the famous Lomonosov Porcelain Factory that stands on the city's outskirts came in to render assistance to the museum. The moment they spotted the old Russian chinaware and the porcelain from all of Europe's best known factories of the past, they at once set to work with a gusto, packing the fragile, unique pieces with the same expertise and skill with which they handled the ware produced at their own factory.

Meanwhile in the chamber whose twenty granite columns had caused it to be styled the Hall of Twenty Columns, the museum's veteran cabinet-makers tirelessly manufactured wedges from unplaned chunks of pinewood to enable the keepers of the Department of Classical Antiquity, along with their sculptor and architect assistants, to pack carefully the black-figure and red-figure vases of old. The handiwork of potters of bygone ages, they had long since come to rest in this realm. The queen of all these wonders was the Regina vasorum. Scholars have emphasized that "the Cumae vase is indeed a unique work of art of ancient times. It is truly remarkable, whether for its exquisite, elegant proportions, its consummate modelling, its blue-black glaze with its metallic sheen, or its profuse decoration. The potter who created it sought to imitate vessels of such precious metals as bronze, silver or gold, as for instance, the silver vase from the Chertomlyk Mound."

The Chertomlyk amphora, which is as famed throughout the world as its regal sister, was being readied for removal in another room of the Department of Classical Antiquity. Its packing, which was a time-consuming process, produced numerous headaches. Though of silver, embossed some twenty-four centuries ago, it is, perhaps, more fragile than millennia-old pottery, Venetian glassware or Sèvres porcelain. To keep it intact, it was decided to fill it to the brim with crumbled cork, as was done with other hollow vessels of fragile and brittle media. However, this was by no means so simple as it may sound. The lower part of this amphora is fitted out with three taps which have strainers soldered on inside across the orifices. One more strainer was soldered on inside across the neck. It was this last strainer that gave the people preparing the Chertomlyk vase for evacuation so much trouble. As the crumbled cork simply refused to pass inside, two of the Hermitage workers were obliged to spend almost half a day feeding teaspoonfuls of cork through a small crack that the ravages of time had wrought near the amphora's lip. Of course the Greek potter cannot be blamed for having been in no position to foresee a contingency whereby his outstanding handiwork would not be filled with the noble juice of the vine; however, three out of every four marble busts of the ancient Roman emperors were crated while the two tired-out ladies continued their manipulations with the teaspoonfuls of crumbled cork.

56, 57

*As soon as the Government announcement of the beginning
of the war was broadcast, the Hermitage rooms became empty.*

The suite of rooms of Italian art in the Old Hermitage
and French art in the Winter Palace

58

Rembrandt. 1606–1669. Holland
The Holy Family

59

*The pride of place
of the Hermitage goes
to the Rembrandt Room.*

The Rembrandt Room
in the New Hermitage
Built by Vasily Stasov
and Nikolai Yefimov after
Leo von Klenze's design.
1842–51

60

*The pictures taken
from their frames
are already packed
in the crates
or rolled on rollers.*

The Rembrandt Room
during the siege
Photograph of 1944

Рембрантовские Голландские залы
Эрмитаже 1942год.

BN
194

In one of the Hermitage rooms the celebrated marble statue of Venus, the Goddess of Love, was being stowed away for removal. This statue, traded by Peter the Great from the Pope for the holy relics of St. Bridget, was also known as the "white she-devil," whose dazzling nudity had thrown fear into the hearts and minds of the bearded boyars. In another, the wax effigy of Peter the Great, which Carlo Rastrelli had sculpted, was likewise being prepared for evacuation. First it was stripped of the parade dress (his cerulean caftan, waistcoat, shirt of fine holland, and breeches the Emperor had worn at the coronation of his spouse, the future Catherine I); then the effigy itself was dismantled into various parts with the wooden elements, the trunk and the upper and lower limbs, and the wax head, feet and hands all packed separately. The respective crates were marked in black letters: "Waxwork effigy! Handle with care!"

Another exhibit that necessitated plenty of labour to ensure its safe removal was the massive one-and-a-half-ton embossed silver sarcophagus of Alexander Nevsky, produced some two hundred years ago at the St. Petersburg Mint, which had been moved after the October Revolution to the Hermitage Museum from the Cathedral of the Alexander Nevsky Monastery. Elsewhere the *Crouching Boy*, the celebrated piece that the great Michelangelo had sculpted four centuries ago for the Medici Chapel in the Florentine Church of San Lorenzo, seemed to bend still lower to squeeze into the double-walled crate that had been made for this work of genius.

By now only the black-stencilled lettering and numbers on the sides of the crates and boxes, enigmatic cyphers for

61

The works of the greatest Dutch artist have been evacuated to the rear, to the Urals...

Vera Miliutina's drawing of the Rembrandt Room during the siege of Leningrad, dated May 1942

62
Rembrandt. 1606–1669. Holland
Flora

63
Rembrandt. 1606–1669. Holland
Portrait of a Scholar

64
Rembrandt. 1606–1669. Holland
The Return of the Prodigal Son

65
Rembrandt. 1606–1669. Holland
The Descent from the Cross

66

68

67

66

The Smaller Skylighted Room during the siege
Photograph of 1944

67

The Smaller Skylighted Room
Drawing by Vasily Kuchumov. 1942

68

The Smaller Skylighted Room in the New Hermitage
Built by Vasily Stasov and Nikolai Yefimov after
Leo von Klenze's design. 1842–51

the layman, that accorded with the description furnished in what might be termed the way bill, designated the objects which but a few days earlier had hung on the walls or stood on the floors of the Hermitage's various galleries and rooms. Now only the evacuation invoices could say which crate contained the etchings of Callot, the Central Asian tiles, the Italian majolica, the Sassanian silver, the statue of the Pharaoh Amonemhat III, Rodin's *Eternal Spring*, the bronze cauldron from Herat, the Fortuny vase, the swords of the Crusaders, the scimitars of the Saracens, the door from the Tomb of Gur-Emir, the bureau made by the German-born cabinet-maker David Roentgen, the ancient vases from Byzantium, the beermugs of medieval Germany, the Coptic textiles, the Flemish tapestries, the Gonzaga cameo, or the tiny female figure carved out of a mammoth tusk, a "Venus of the Stone Age." Yes, now the way bill became a kind of Hermitage catalogue.

69

In the Picture Gallery, all the canvases had been packed except one that continued to hang in its frame in its customary place. That was Rembrandt's *Descent from the Cross*. It was so large that it needed to be rolled round a roller, but it was feared that this operation, not the best way to handle a painting in any case, might irretrievably damage both the canvas and the paint. A special council was called of the most distinguished experts in the art of restoration. These were people who knew all there was to know about many of the Old Masters in the Hermitage collection, not only as immortal works of genius, but as objects susceptible to the ravages of time, masterpieces which they had done their utmost to preserve for future admiration. They now had to decide whether the rolling-up technique would damage this Rembrandtian gem or not. After much deliberation and after weighing all the

70

TITIANVS . P.

71

69

Titian. 1485/90–1576. Italy
Danaë

70

Titian. 1485/90–1576. Italy
Portrait of a Woman

71

Titian. 1485/90–1576. Italy
St Mary Magdalene in Penitence

the war broke out, before going out to fight, many joined that force dedicated to saving the treasures of the Hermitage, which as the illustrious Soviet poet Nikolai Tikhonov, chronicler of war-time Leningrad, recalled later, was directed by the ubiquitous Academician Orbeli. Orbeli seemed to be everywhere at once, garbed in his blue smock, with bits of cotton wool on sleeves and trouser legs and with shavings and sawdust spattered over his unruly beard.

The last object to be carted away was Houdon's *Voltaire*. The illustrious French philosopher seemed to raise himself up from the arm-rests of his chair when the seamen marched in to carry him downstairs. No doubt he would have risen to full stature and descended to board the coach awaiting outside if not for the marble heaviness of his frail body.

The seamen in their dungarees placed runners under the marble chair and rolled the statue up to the top of the New Hermitage's Main Staircase; next, employing a system of ropes and pulleys, they let the massive figure roll slowly down the wooden planking covering all three flights of steps. As the seamen strained their muscles to hold the statue in place, there came down the steps alongside of them that stooped-shouldered gentleman with the tangled beard and with the bits of fluff sticking to his blue smock.

In the vestibule Voltaire's "coach," the immense crate with the statue already deposited inside, was sealed and entered into the way bill. Around midnight a lorry drove up and backed up onto the pavement, its tailgate almost touching the toes of the granite atlantes outside the main entrance. One after another, lorries, piled high with sealed crates and containers, rolled away under armed escort to the railway goods depot.

The gems of the Hermitage collection were deposited in an armoured car. Other special treasures were loaded into four-axle Pullmans. Besides its twenty-two goods cars, this special-purpose train had

In a few days the packed exhibits will be in the faraway town of Sverdlovsk in the Urals.
Crates with the Hermitage treasures in Sverdlovsk. Photograph of 1941

boxes, the army command despatched a small force of naval ratings and soldiers.

It should be noted that generally the men of the Red Army and Navy serving in and around Leningrad were no strangers to the Hermitage. In conformity with a well-established tradition of years' standing, each Sunday groups of soldiers and sailors would march up to the museum to join the usual influx of visitors and spend several hours listening to the Hermitage guide on the excursions around the museum. No wonder, when

pros and cons, they finally unanimously decided that it could be done and must be done.

Thus one more empty frame was returned to its original place as had been done with every such frame after the picture it had previously enclosed had been removed. As a result, towards the close of the week, row upon row, tier upon tier of empty frames filled the walls, often right up to the ceiling — except for a few blank spots in the rooms devoted to Italian art, where there had hung a number of devotional images painted on wooden panels. Not removed from their frames were those three gems created by the geniuses whose names are Leonardo da Vinci and Raphael Santi, notably the *Benois Madonna*, also known as the *Madonna with a Flower*, the *Litta Madonna* and the *Conestabile Madonna*.

As was noticed earlier, as soon as a crate was nailed up it would be dragged downstairs closer to the doors and gates. Some weighed as much as a ton, if not more, others less, while some, though seemingly small in size, could be extremely heavy, especially if they contained coins or medals. To lug and move all these massive and not so massive crates and

73

72, 73

The Greater Skylighted Room
in the New Hermitage
Built by Vasily Stasov and Nikolai Yefimov
after Leo von Klenze's design. 1842–51

74

another two cars, one for the Hermitage staff accompanying the museum's treasures on their long journey east and the other for the armed escort, plus two open platforms at either end, upon which were mounted anti-aircraft guns and machine-guns, their muzzles pointing skywards.

The train pulled out of the goods depot at daybreak on July 1 — however, without the traditional whistle, as ever since June 27, for four days then, locomotives and factories were allowed to blow their hooters for one sole purpose — to announce an air-raid alert. Two engines pulled the train along, while a third went ahead to clear the tracks. Now and again the train halted but always some distance from railway station platforms, and armed sentinels were posted immediately on every side. Soldiers free from sentry duty would rush off to the stations to buy the newspapers. The war communiqués were disheartening and it seemed as if the frontlines were coming closer to Leningrad than was actually the case; the only consolation was that half a million of the Hermitage's most prized treasures were already out of immediate danger. The train pulled into the railway station of Sverdlovsk on the morning of July 6 and unloading commenced at once, with the steel-plated goods car assuming priority.

At the Hermitage a second stage of removal was initiated, with crates again knocked together, this time to take the million-odd items that were usually not on regular display, although they too were worthwhile works of art. The half-million-odd exhibits evacuated eastwards to Sverdlovsk had even exceeded the number envisaged by the evacuation programme. But now it was vital to send away virtually everything of the Hermitage collections, items that were seen by the public, as a rule, only during one or another special exhibition. The drastic worsening of the situation at the fighting fronts was responsible for this new decision.

Hitler and his generals regarded the speedy capture of Leningrad as vital to their plans for a lightning war. Field Marshal von Leeb's armour thrust towards Leningrad and already stood on its distant approaches. To help the Red Army contain the enemy offensive, men of the most peaceful pursuits rallied by the thousands to join the People's Volunteers and trained in the city's streets and squares.

Many of the Hermitage staff also volunteered for the front. Meanwhile those who were too old or too weak continued as before to pack everything that could be packed, or, by way of precaution against possible fires, lugged sacks of sand up to the attics and into the halls and galleries.

Pigeons still billed and cooed on the windowsills. There came through the windows opening onto Palace Square the stamping of marching feet and the shouts of military commands; companies of the People's Volunteers were taking a crash course of training in the basics of hand-to-hand fighting and anti-tank techniques. Meanwhile one could hear through the museum's windows facing the courtyard the screeching and knocking of handsaws and hammers; crates were being hastily knocked together down in the inner quadrangle. As no time could be lost it was thought better to do this right on the spot.

Again, as during the first evacuation week, the Hermitage's numerous friends rallied to its aid, helping to pack the second batch of museum treasures, with other artists and architects taking over from those who had enlisted in the fighting forces or the People's Volunteers and who were currently going through the crash training in Palace Square. As for those Hermitage workers who had gone to the front, their places were taken by those museum researchers whom the war had summoned back from far-away field expeditions.

Among those returning from a field party out in Armenia, where he had been in charge of the team of archaeologists excavating the Karmir Blur, or Red Hill site, in the vicinity of Yerevan, the republic's capital, was Professor Boris Piotrovsky. He was then thirty-three years old, and today is the Director of the Hermitage with a string of titles to his credit: besides his Full Membership in the USSR and Armenian Academies of Sciences, he is a Fellow or Honorary Member of numerous scientific societies and associations abroad. Indeed, it was on the slopes of Karmir Blur that almost thirty years earlier, on the eve of the First World War, the then young Iosif Orbeli — later the celebrated Academician Orbeli, the selfsame Orbeli who was the Hermitage Director and Piotrovsky's

77

El Greco. 1541–1614. Spain
St Peter and St Paul

78

Diego Velázquez. 1599–1660. Spain
Luncheon

mentor — initiated the search for relics of the ancient state of Urartu, whose domain back in the ninth — sixth centuries B.C. had stretched across the Armenian foothills, including part that is incorporated in the present Soviet Republic of Armenia. However, the fates so ordained that the gods of ancient Urartu were more condescending to Piotrovsky than to his teacher, as in 1939 he uncovered beneath the reddish clay the remains of the ancient Urartian citadel of Teičebaini, with the result that the first finds, precious relics of an ancient culture, which spend-thrift humanity had long forgotten, now graced the Hermitage collections.

However, towards the close of June 1941, a few days after the war had broken out, Professor Piotrovsky called a complete halt to all further excavation on Karmir Blur and returned to Leningrad. At the outset, the

79
The Van Dyck Room in the New Hermitage
Built by Vasily Stasov and Nikolai Yefimov
after Leo von Klenze's design. 1842–51

80
Piles of sand and shovels were seen everywhere.
The Van Dyck Room during the siege of Leningrad
Drawing by Vasily Kuchumov. 1942

sight that met him at the Hermitage reminded him somewhat of the fuss and bustle of a large archaeological field expedition getting ready to break camp and move, lock, stock and barrel, as everywhere he saw artifacts strewn in haphazard confusion and being packed by his colleagues from the Caucasus Department, and everywhere were piles of sand with that customary tool of the archaeologist, the spade, thrust in them in great number.

As always after a long absence, the first thing he did upon his return to the Hermitage was to look for the Urartian relics that he had earlier, in pre-war times, despatched to the museum. However,

81

82

83

81

The suite of rooms in the Winter Palace
displaying French art
Designed by Alexander Briullov. 1839

82, 83

*The paintings are evacuated; vases, torchères,
and table-tops are stowed away under the heavy
vaults of the ground floor.*

Drawings by Vasily Kuchumov. 1942

the showcases were empty; all that met his eyes were dark patches on the faded cloth, some round, others oval and still others rectangular, the traces of the trophies he knew so well, the artifacts that he himself had unearthed on Karmir Blur. But they were gone — and along with them were the objects that had once graced the showcases in the other rooms and halls. It was as if the very soul had been plucked out of them. Now, there was nothing but an emptiness, aching voids, with the staff engaged in totally different jobs than had been their occupation before the war. Now Boris

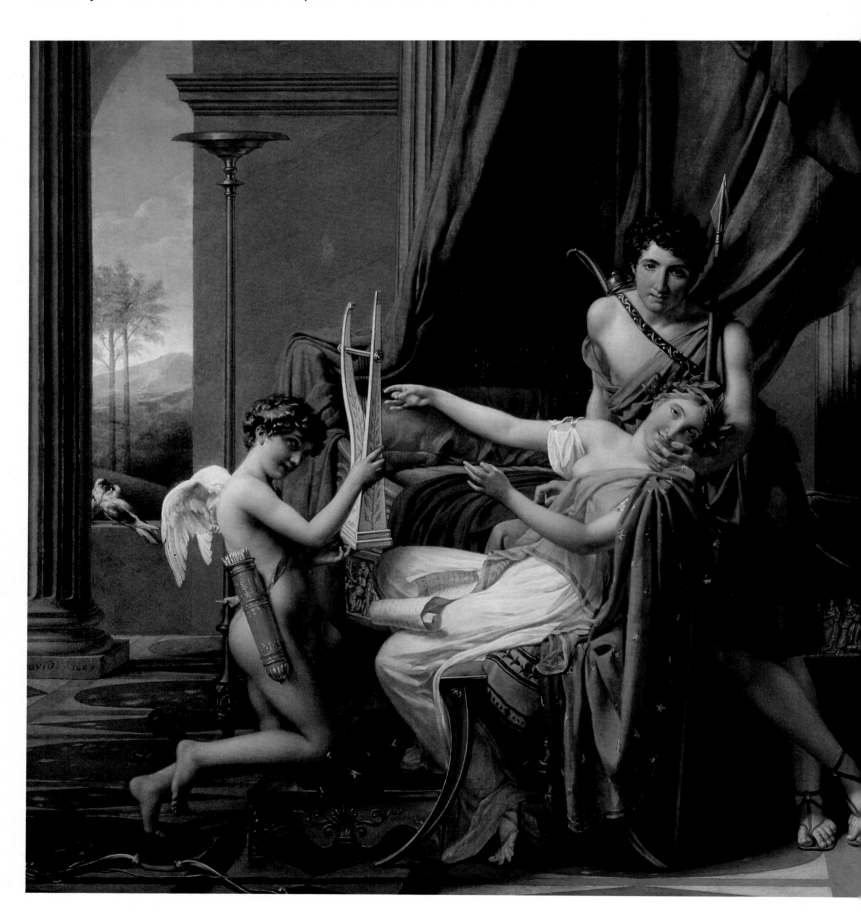

Piotrovsky did not know where to turn and what to look for, everything was so strange. His initial sense of dismay and confusion did not last very long though. A half hour later he bumped into the Director, from whom he gathered what was happening and what he should do; still earlier he had already learned at the local ARP centre that he had been appointed the deputy chief of the Hermitage fire-warden team.

By mid-July Leningrad was directly menaced. Pskov, 276 kilometres from the city, had been taken and Nazi forces had neared Kingisepp, 137 kilometres distant, Novgorod, 204 kilometres distant, and Luga, 139 kilometres away. Fierce fighting was in process on the Karelian Isthmus north of the city. Now air-raid alerts were more and more frequent. However, amidst it all the Hermitage staff continued to pack museum treasures for the second evacuation train, and like their fellow-townsmen, did everything that the war effort demanded of them, fitting out air-raid shelters, or going

86
The Room of 18th-century
English Art in the Winter Palace
Designed by Alexander Briullov. 1839

87
Castors and cruets
England
By Augustine Courtauld. 1741–42

88
Bowl for punch
England
By Gabriel Smith. 1710–11

89
Samovar
England
By Charles Wright. 1770–71

out to dig trenches and put up anti-tank barriers at Luga and Kingisepp or racing off to their assigned posts as ARP wardens the moment the air-raid alert was sounded.

And again convoys of trucks rolled up to the Hermitage doors to take the massive, heavy crates that the members of the People's Volunteers helped to load, replacing the seamen who had earlier trundled the marble statue of Voltaire down the staircase.

The second evacuation train pulled out of Leningrad on July 20. It carried away in its twenty-three goods vans a total of four hundred and twenty-two crates containing more than seven hundred thousand Hermitage works of art.

The Hermitage's staff busied themselves packing what was left for a third evacuation train. On the main notice board now appeared announcements of the first deaths of the Hermitage workers killed in action. Along with these mournful notices were the War Bulletins — of the same type as were put out by the men in the trenches, aboard warships and at military

87

88   89

90

Silver dish showing
Shapur II hunting
Persia. 4th century

91

Bronze bucket
from Herat.
Persia.
12th century

92

*By now only
the numbers
on the sides
of the crates and
boxes designated
the objects that
but a few days
earlier had been
displayed in
the rooms and halls
of the Hermitage.*

Boxes with
Hermitage
treasures
are prepared
for evacuation

90

airfields. The Hermitage bulletins summoned all who could of the staff to go out to the suburbs of the city to dig trenches, put up anti-tank entanglements, and build pill-boxes and other fortifications.

Every day hundreds of thousands of Leningraders contributed to the defence effort and among them were always some thirty or forty members of the Hermitage Museum staff. This, however, presented a difficult problem, as what the Hermitage staff could not brag of was physical stamina and energy; no wonder, as most were well past the prime of life.

In their sun-bleached shirts and blouses, in mud-spattered overalls, with rucksacks slung over their backs and with crowbars and shovels in hand, the museum staff, faces blackened by the filth and the scorching sun, returned to the Hermitage, where they were again to pack and wrap and carefully stash and stow away all that was necessary in the hastily knocked-together crates and boxes.

"That was a tough phase of evacuation," Professor Miliza Matie, the Egyptologist, who was then the Deputy Director of the Hermitage responsible for research work, but who at the time was

93

in charge exclusively of evacuation procedures, recalled later. "Indeed, perhaps it was the toughest thing ever done at the time. Truth to tell, however great the effort invested to despatch the first June train and second July one, in August it seemed to me that the getting ready of those two trains had been just a run-of-the-mill affair."

As was said earlier, contingency evacuation plans had been made long before the outbreak of war and it seemed that everything that could possibly be needed had been provided for. However, the fact remained that to get ready the two evacuation trains that had gone east, the Hermitage had used up fifty tons of shavings, three tons of cotton wool and sixteen kilometres of oil-cloth. At any rate, by August all stores of packaging materials had been exhausted. True, planking was still available, but by this time there were no carpenters left. Professor Miliza Matie and other scholars of the Hermitage Museum staff

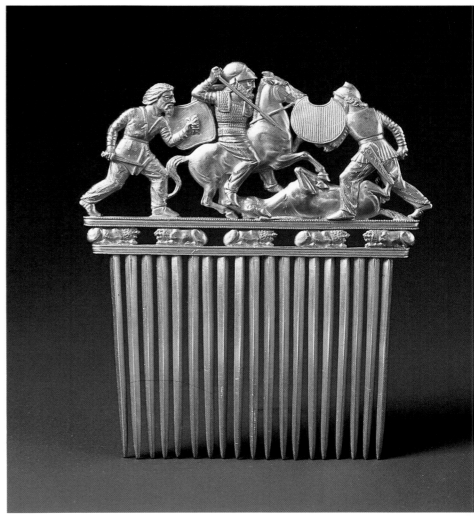

94   95

93

Though the statue of Pallas Athena wrought by Phidias is irrevocably lost, the face of the Greek Goddess re-created by an anonymous goldsmith continues to adorn the gold pendants found during the excavations of the Kul-Oba barrow.

Temple pendant with the head of Athena Parthenos (one of a pair). Athens. Phidias's workshop (?), 5th century B.C.

94

Gold deer. 6th century B.C.

95

Gold comb from the Solokha barrow. 4th century B.C.

96

Vessel from the Kul-Oba barrow. 4th century B.C.

97

Scythian gold glows and sparkles in the showcases of the Gold Room, which possesses one of the richest collections of Scythian art in the world.

Scythian gold, which is included in Peter the Great's Siberian Collection

98

The unique pieces from the Siberian collection of Peter the Great are shown together with the gold objects found in the burial grounds in the south of Russia.

The Novocherkassk treasures

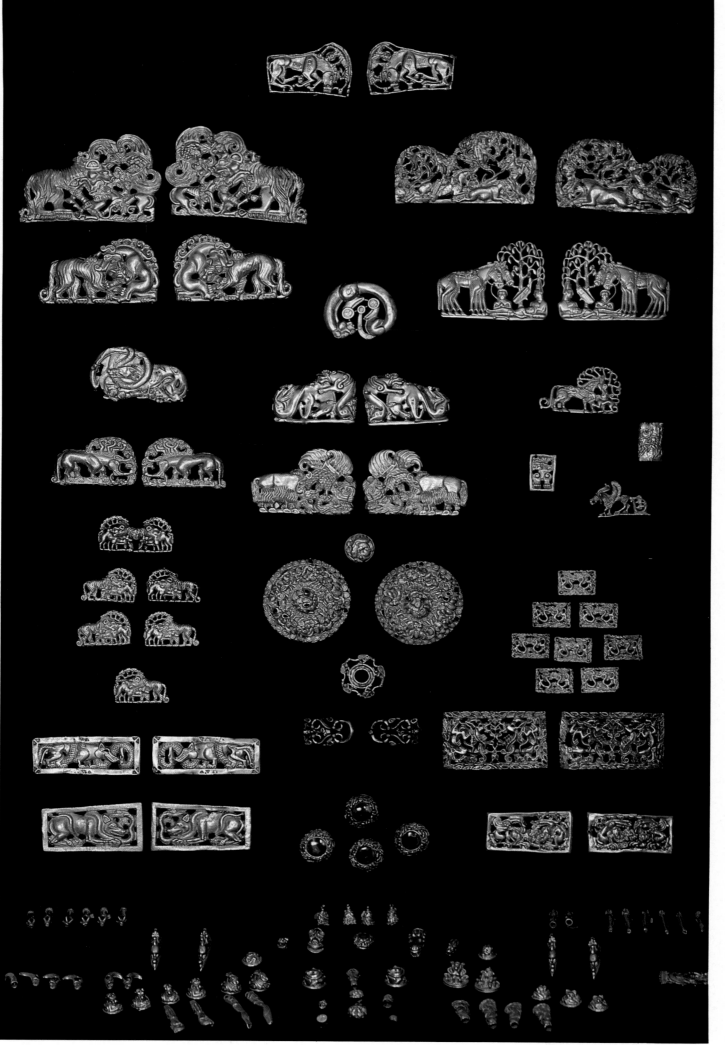

spent hours on the phone ringing sundry food stores and shops to find out whether they could offer any boxes of wood or cardboard, in short anything that might serve as packaging.

Three hundred and fifty-one crates had been nailed up for the third evacuation train, when, on August 30, Director of the Hermitage Museum, Iosif Orbeli, suddenly announced that all the work should be halted. It appeard that the day

99

*The Gold Room of the Hermitage Museum
displays a brilliant collection of jewellery
of the seventeenth, eighteenth and
nineteenth centuries.
It took only a few minutes to wrap each piece
in tissue paper but there were more than
ten thousand rings alone to be wrapped.*

Rings and brooches
Russia, France, Germany. 17th–18th centuries

100

Chatelaine watches decorated with precious stones
France, Switzerland. 18th century

101

Snuff-boxes decorated with precious stones
England, Germany, Russia. 18th century

102

Bouquet of precious stones
Russia. 1740

before Nazi forces had straddled the last of the open railway lines which were linking the city with the hinterland. Yet in the morning two trains had managed to bypass Mga station, which Nazi armour had captured around noon. Cluttering up all the tracks of the Leningrad railway hub were more than two thousand goods vans and cars loaded with the property of many of the city's enterprises and offices. The crated Hermitage items, which had been prepared for the third evacuation train, had not even covered the short distance to the goods depot, and remained behind on the ground floor filling up the entire area between the twin rows of gleaming white columns of Rastrelli's famous gallery, right up to the glittering railings of the lowest flight of the Main Staircase.

Thus, by early September 1941, Nazi forces had completely encircled the city from the south and southwest and from the north. On September 4, Nazi long-range artillery shelled Leningrad, while two days later, on September 6, enemy aircraft broke through to bomb the besieged city for the first time. When the old fortress of Schlüsselburg at the mouth of the Neva was captured,

Leningrad was completely cut off by land and water, as shipping on the Neva came to a standstill. The first day of the nine-hundred-day siege had dawned.

On that day of September 8 Nazi bombers staged two massive raids. The aircraft that appeared over Leningrad at five minutes to seven in the early evening rained down a total of 6,327 incendiary bombs causing fires — 178 all told — to break out in all sections of the city. Fire-fighting was still continuing when at 10:35 p.m. waves of heavy bombers came over to drop high-explosive bombs.

The Hermitage ARP command was alerted a little before seven o'clock. At eleven o'clock at night a powerful explosion rocked the Palace Embankment. A high-explosive bomb had hit a block of flats on the embankment right next door to the Hermitage. Its ARP wardens were summoned to the spot. In the light of the moon they saw that the entire front wall had caved in, opening up the

gruesome spectacle of domestic intimacy stripped of all privacy. In one place a lampshade swayed in the wind, in another a picture hung askew over a settee, in a third a child's raincoat dangled on a clothes rack in the hallway. Equipped with first-aid kits, helmeted and gloved in canvas gauntlets, the museum ARP wardens cleared away the heaps of broken brick and the remains of charred flooring and helped to dig out the living and the dead and bandage the wounded.

The next night another eighteen enemy bombers broke through the city's anti-aircraft defences. Again the Hermitage ARP wardens raced up to the attics and rooftops and to respective stations on the stairs and in the halls, whose dirtied parquet floors were still littered with

105

106

straggling scraps of paper and wisps of cotton wool, which were the traces of the so recent evacuation effort.

Now the Hermitage staff spent most of the time as ARP wardens on the museum's rooftops: enemy bombing raids became more frequent and longer in duration. On the rooftops, too, besides the ARP wardens who were ever prepared to extinguish an incendiary were the spotters who took their posts on the observation platforms. One such platform had been erected above the Winter Palace's Armorial Hall, and another by the large skylights of the New Hermitage, which served to illuminate the central halls of the Picture Gallery below. The task before the spotters was to report the outbreak of fires within the zone of visibility.

"We underwent our baptism of fire during the first few days of the siege, when Nazi aircraft staged massive bombing raids on the city," Hermitage ARP wardens, who had also worked as spotters, recalled after the war. "Bombs burst, explosions thundered and the ack-ack guns roared. Luckily no bombs came down upon us; however, flying fragments did scorch through the roof-top. Fortunately we escaped unscathed, as we watched the numerous fires which were blazing in those parts of the city that we could see."

No longer did the pigeons coo on the windowsills. They left the palace eaves, where they had nested before, for strange parts, where no bombs burst, no shells whistled past, no guns thundered. The acrid fumes of gunpowder and smoke now filled the Hermitage and at night the blood-red glare of the fires gleamed on the parquet mosaics and on the cold marble of the walls, and was reflected back in multiple images in the ceiling-high palace mirrors.

By now the Nazi troops had occupied Peterhof (now Petrodvorets) and Pushkin, in the suburbs of the city.

108

Persian ceramics. 17th century

109

Crates with the exhibits of the Oriental Department
Photograph of 1941

110

Tile
Persia. 17th century

111

Room of Persian Art in the Winter Palace
(The Blue Hall)

112

Unknown Chinese artist.
15th – first half of the 17th century
Portrait of an Official and His Wife

113

Buddha Amida Meeting the Soul
of a Righteous Man
China. 12th century

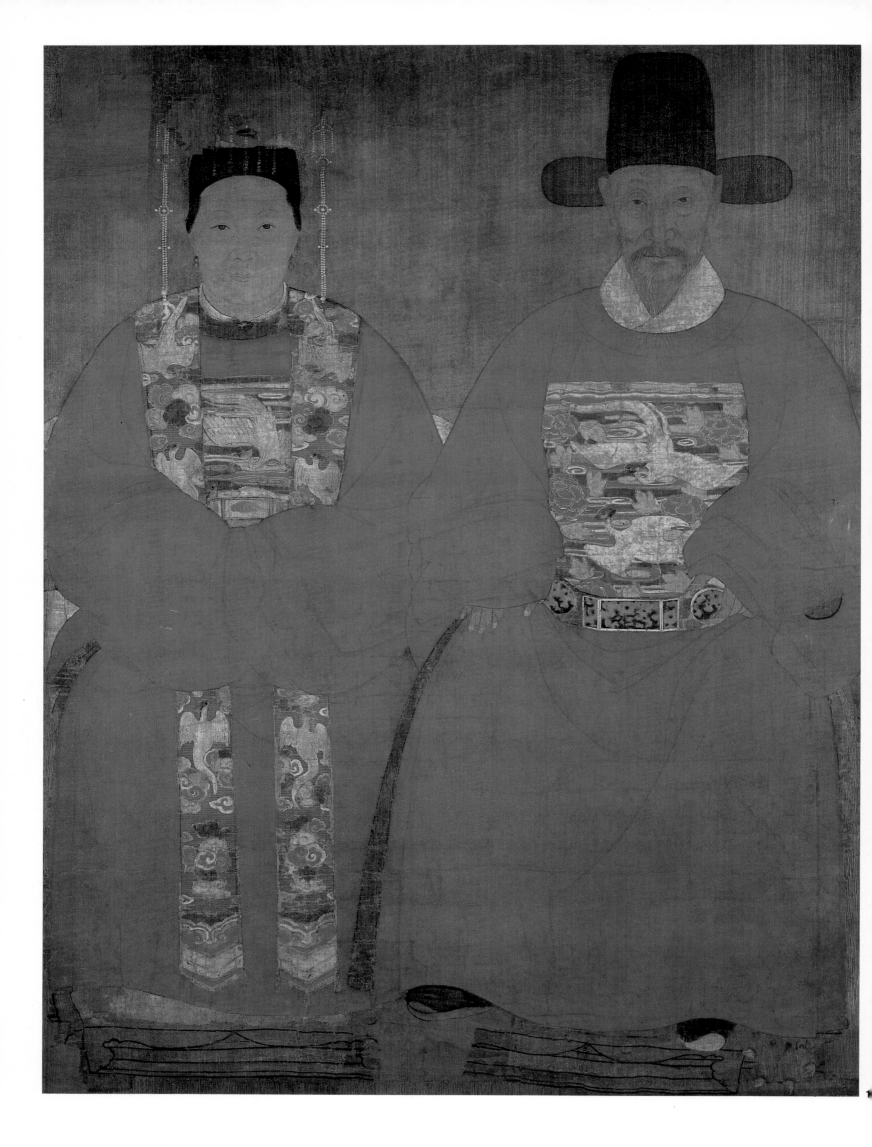

Leningraders girded themselves for street fighting. The squares, avenues and embankments bristled with anti-tank and anti-infantry entanglements. Houses were transformed into pillboxes and windows into embrasures. As Palace Square was thought a likely spot for an enemy paratroop landing, machine-guns were mounted on the rooftops of the nearby buildings, including the Hermitage. However, shortly afterwards they were removed by order of the Leningrad Front Command. They were likewise removed from the rooftops of other historic buildings, in hope of protecting Leningrad's art monuments from damage and destruction.

The moon that now illumined the city during the nights could not peep into all of the Hermitage Museum's windows. Boarded up from inside were

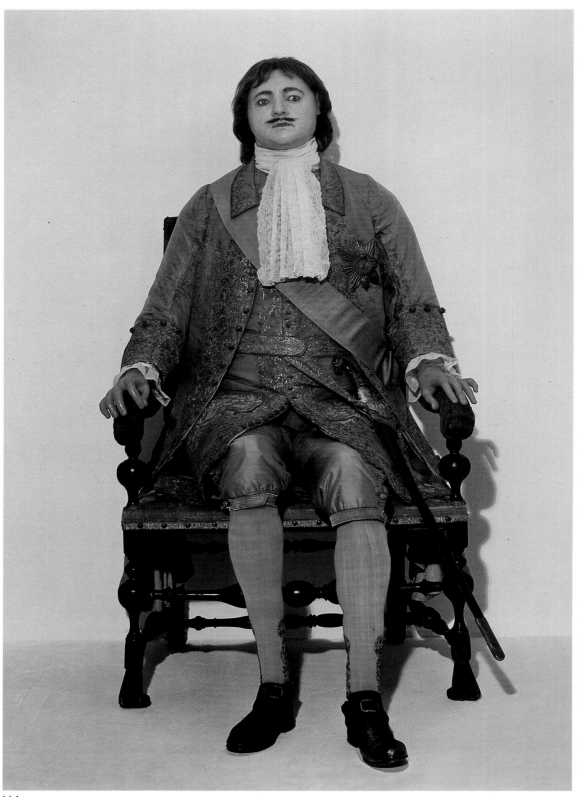

114

Wax effigy of Peter the Great
Russia. 18th century

115

*In one of the Hermitage rooms
the celebrated marble statue
of Venus, bought in the days
of Peter the Great,
was being packed;
in another, the wax effigy
of Peter the Great, made by
Carlo Rastrelli, father
of the architect who designed
the Winter Palace, was likewise
prepared for evacuation.*

Venus of Taurida
Roman copy after a Greek original
of the 3rd century B.C.

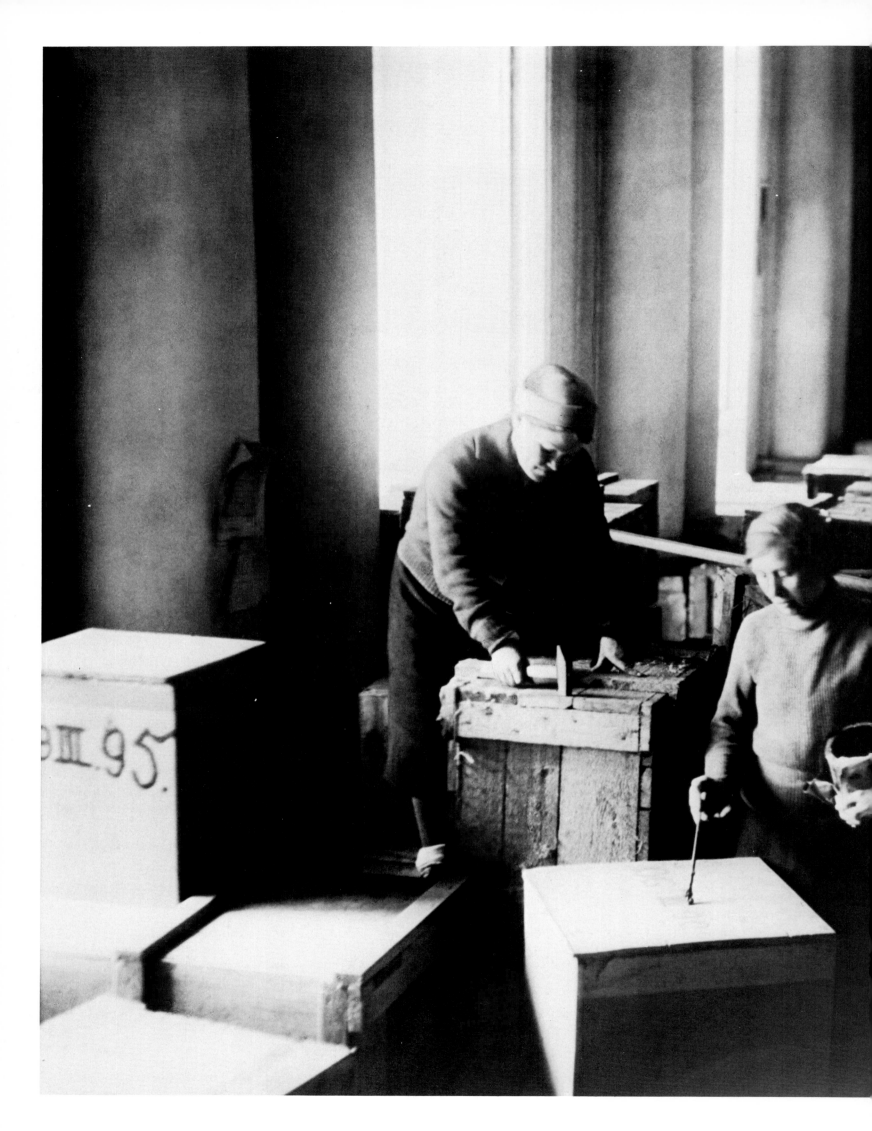

all thirteen windows — overlooking the Winter Canal — of the Raphael Loggias, that glassed arcade which the architect Quarenghi had built in the eighteenth century in imitation of the celebrated loggias of the Vatican Palace. The paintings covering the walls and ceilings of this gallery reproduce, with an amazingly faithful accuracy, the inimitable frescoes that the great master had executed for the loggias in the Vatican. During the 250 years that they adorned the gallery (since the reign of the Empress Catherine the Great), these unique copies, made in the eighteenth century after Raphael's originals, which had regrettably begun to decay, were taken down but once — in the mid-nineteenth century, when the building of the New Hermitage that was to incorporate the loggias was constructed. It appeared most hazardous to once again remove the canvases and roll them onto rollers and, hence, they remained on the walls. The thirteen windows of Quarenghi's gallery, however, were carefully boarded up with thick planking from within, and this was further reinforced by bags of sand which were stacked up to the very top.

Likewise the authentic fresco that the artist-monk Fra Angelico had painted exactly five hundred years earlier was left untouched. Done in the early 1440s in watercolours on damp plaster for the Monastery of San Domenico outside Florence, it was removed from the wall of the refectory and brought to St. Petersburg towards the close of the nineteenth century, at which time it was attached to the Hermitage wall by means

116

Marking the boxes before the evacuation
Photograph of 1941

117

Lebes with toilet scenes
Attica. 4th century B.C.

118

Red-figure psykter with a scene of
feasting hetaerae
Attica. By master Euphronios.
C. 505–500 B.C.

119

Red-figure pelike with a swallow
Attica. Euphronios's workshop. *C.* 510 B.C.

118

117

119

of the ground floor and of the palace basements were massive enough to withstand the destructive power of the biggest blockbuster bomb and the largest artillery shell.

The members of the museum staff now became movers and riggers. They brought down from the top floors to the safest possible places thousands of items that had been in the museum reserves and remained unpacked. Among them were heavy marble and bronze objects and elegant pieces of furniture. As for the table tops, torchères and massive vases of malachite, lapis lazuli, porphyry and jasper, everything that could be dismantled was taken apart and brought down to the ground floor piece by piece.

The rooms in the Department of Classical Antiquity that after the evacuation effort in June and July were empty, now offered refuge and shelter from bombs and shells for the semi-precious stones from the Urals fashioned

128, 129

Hydria from Cumae:
Regina vasorum
Campania.
Late 4th century B.C.

120

120

Oinochoe in the form of a woman's head
Attica. By master Charin.
Late 6th century B.C.

121

Kylix
Attica. By master Psiax.
C. 500 B.C.

122

Lekane with toilet scenes
Attica. 4th century B.C.

of iron clamps. As it was rightly deemed that its removal and transportation would damage this five-hundred-year-old fresco beyond repair, it was decided to erect a breastwork of sand four metres wide and three metres high, further reinforced by planking on every side — in the room where Fra Angelico's creation had always been exhibited — between it and the windows that looked out onto the Neva and whose sole protection from the shock waves and flying bomb fragments was the strips of paper glued crosswise onto the panes of glass.

Several other unique pieces, whose fragility or excessive ponderousness made even their removal to a safer place within the Hermitage itself, let alone evacuation, completely out of the question, were kept in place in the first-floor rooms. Everything else that had not been evacuated in time was hastily carried down into the ground-floor rooms and cellars. The army experts who had been summoned to the Hermitage to make the necessary calculations unanimously concluded that the vaulting and walls

123

Krater
Attica. *C.* 500 B.C.

124

Hydria showing Achilles
tying Hector's body to the chariot
Attica. By Master of Antiope. *C.* 510 B.C.

121

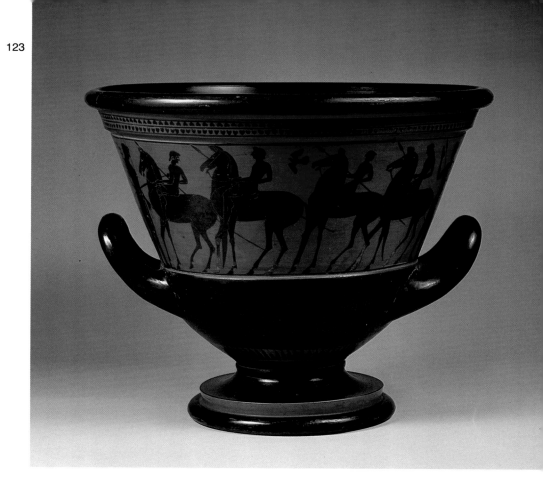

123

124

122

125

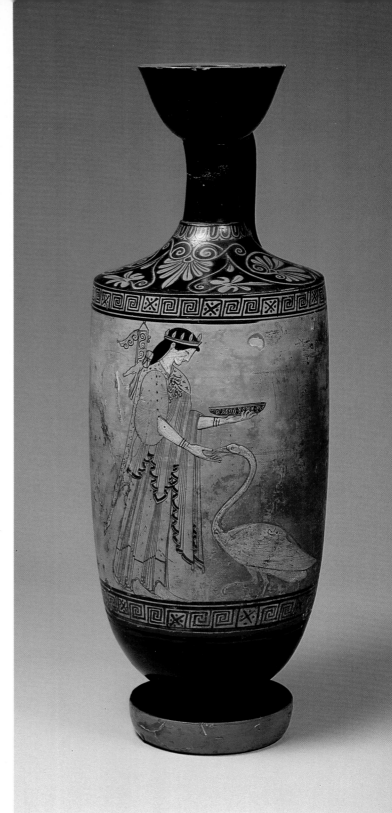

127

126

125

Figure vessel in the form of a sphinx
Attica. Late 5th century B.C.

126

Lekythos with a scene of a boar hunt
Athens. By master Xenophantos.
4th century B.C.

127

Lekythos
Attica. By Master of Pan. *C.* 490 B.C.

130

The Hall of Twenty Columns.
Detail of wall painting

131

*The Hall of Twenty Columns
in the New Hermitage
had long been the realm
of antique vases.*

The Hall of Twenty Columns
in the New Hermitage
Built by Vasily Stasov
and Nikolai Yefimov
after Leo von Klenze's
design. 1842–51

by Russian craftsmen, for the stacks of paintings which in the room devoted to the statue of Jupiter now clustered around the empty pedestals of the evacuated statues of deities and Roman emperors, and for the medieval halberds and pikes which had been lowered down the steep inner stairway straight from the Hermitage armoury into the room known as the Hall of the Swan. Meanwhile, all porcelain that had been left behind was carried down into the cellar beneath the room where the statue of Athena had been on display.

To this end the cellar's stone floor was covered with a layer of sand, taken from the mound that had piled up in one of the Hermitage's inner courtyards in the early days of the war. It had been brought in by barge up the Neva and into the Winter Canal. Subsequently the museum staff and undergraduates of the Leningrad Conservatoire and Academy of Arts, who had helped to unload the barge, trundled it up to all floors and attics — twenty-eight metres high — of the palace. Thus, whereas the items that had been evacuated east had been carefully packed in cotton wool, the museum porcelain left behind was half buried in the sand on the floor of the Hermitage cellar.

On the night of September 18, during the Nazi shelling of the city, which had continued uninterruptedly for as long as a fortnight now, an artillery shell burst right outside the Hermitage Museum entrance embellished by the granite atlantes, near the bridge spanning the Winter Canal. The sizzling splinters pocked the brick walls and in the Athena Hall the shock wave blasted to smithereens all the window panes crisscrossed with glued-on strips of paper. Those ladies on the museum staff, who that very morning had been occupied with their porcelain in the cellar below, at once raced down the stairs to inspect their precious collection. As they switched on the light they saw protruding from the bed of sand, completely unruffled, the flirtatious marquises with their languorous cavaliers, the dainty shepherdesses, the vases with their Rococo scroll-work, and the chandeliers. Literally every piece was intact: the cups, the coffee pots, the plates, the tureens, the saltcellars; indeed it seemed that a banquet table with covers for a thousand persons was laid in that cellar.

Meanwhile, overhead, in the Athena Hall, the splinters of glass were swept away from the mosaic floor that had in its time been recovered from excavations of ancient Chersonesus, near Sevastopol in the Crimea, and delivered to the Hermitage in the past century. The empty windows were boarded up with the first set of plywood sheets to "adorn" the museum.

Nazi long-range artillery shelled the city round the clock and enemy aerial bombardments continued night after night. Enemy encirclement throttled the city in an ever tighter grip. Now Leningraders took not the suburban trains but the municipal tramcars to reach the new defensive fortifications being hastily built round their home town. Von Leeb's forces were only six kilometres away from the Kirov Metal Works, one of the city's oldest industrial enterprises, and but fourteen kilometres from Palace Square, the Winter Palace and the Hermitage. A mere fourteen kilometres! It has been estimated that to see everything there is to see in the Hermitage, the visitor must cover a total distance of twenty-two kilometres. And now but fourteen kilometres remained from the front lines to the Hermitage!

On the night of September 21 an urgent summons was sent out to all factories and offices still operating in the city. The Hermitage warden posted by the telephone logged:

"Tomorrow, September 22, 1941, at 10 a.m., all able-bodied members of the Hermitage staff are to report to the Kirov District for work on the construction of defensive fortifications. Half the ARP team are to stay at their posts."

Those were the decisive days of the Nazi assault. Each and every Leningrader considered him or herself mobilized as a member of the civilian garrison holding their home town.

Meanwhile the civilian garrison of the Hermitage maintained their ARP vigil in the museum's rooms and on its rooftops. They left only to exchange places with their fellow ARP wardens and march those fourteen kilometres to the front lines, there to pitch in with fellow-townsmen building an impregnable line of fortifications close to the Kirov Works and just outside the Narva Gates on the city's outskirts.

Then, on October 7 Hitler despatched from his headquarters a new directive to the generals commanding the Nazi forces beleaguering Leningrad. The basic idea was to destroy the city

132

The Chertomlyk vase was prepared for the evacuation with particular care. Though of silver embossed some twenty-four centuries ago, it became more fragile than millennia-old pottery, Venetian glassware or Sèvres porcelain.

Silver amphora from the Chertomlyk barrow.
4th century B.C.

133

The marble statue of the Crouching Boy *seemed to bend still lower when it was being placed in the double-walled crate made for it.*

Michelangelo. 1475–1564
Italy
The Crouching Boy

134

Room of frescoes of the Raphael school in the New Hermitage
Built by Vasily Stasov and Nikolai Yefimov after Leo von Klenze's design. 1842–51

135

Room of frescoes of the Raphael school
Photograph of 1944

136

Repository of Western
European Sculpture
War-time photograph

137

Prosper d'Epinay. 1836–1912
France
Cupid Begging Alms

138

Bertel Thorvaldsen. 1770–1844
Denmark
Cupid and Anacreon

136

137

completely, as it was obvious that the attempt to take the city by assault had failed. On their way from the Nieman to the Neva and at the walls of Leningrad the Nazis had lost in action more than 190,000 men and a veritable legion of tanks, guns and aircraft. Though the Soviet troops holding the city had sustained heavy casualties, they had not been beaten. Within the grip of the blockade they resembled a steel coil compressed to the utmost and ever ready to lash out at the enemy with tremendous force. Leningrad kept at bay at its walls an enemy force of 300,000 strong.

Hitler and his generals now hoped to wear down the resistance put up by Leningrad's gallant defenders. Through the hunger and cold of a protracted, harsh and cruel siege, they attempted to reduce this sprawling metropolis to a heap of rubble by never-ending shelling and aerial bombardment. "The Führer has ordered the city of Petersburg to be wiped off the face of the earth," said the directive issued to the generals laying siege to Leningrad.

In September 1941, 5,364 shells were fired at the city and 16,087 high-explosive and incendiary bombs were dropped on it. In the following month of October the figures were still higher, 7,590 and 44,102 respectively. The bread ration had been cut three times; on October 1, factory workers received a daily ration of 400 grammes and all others half that. Reserves of fuel were likewise running out; the days grew shorter and colder; at dusk, owing to electricity shortages most houses were wrapped in complete darkness.

During the short autumn days and in the breaks between the air-raid alerts, the Hermitage staff continued to stow the objects of art away in relative safety beneath the vaulting of the ground floor and cellars; meanwhile during the long autumn nights, the researchers, again during the breaks between the air-raid alerts, descended from the pocked and pitted rooftops and turned to affairs that had long since been their basic occupation in life. Pulling out the drawers of their desks, they extracted therefrom the manuscripts of unfinished studies and treatises. Above their heads the electric lamps glowed dimly. Often they went out and then, huddling in the darkness, the staff would reminisce and reflect and at times wonder whether more waves of Heinckels and Junkers would come over that night.

Depicted in black and white on a sheet of drawing paper is the spire of the Peter and Paul Fortress, barely discernible in the black void; searchlight beams stab the black skies overhead in which

138

artillery shells are bursting; churning up sprays of cascading rubble, high-explosive bombs burst on the dark ground as buildings cave in and walls collapse. In the lower half of this black-and-white drawing that so well reproduces the atmosphere of the war-time nights of Leningrad, a patch of light is banded by a semi-circle of two parallel lines. Within it we see an elderly man in a padded jacket leaning over a draughtsman's board. The sloping, vaulted ceiling of the cellar in which the draughtsman has taken shelter bears the words that Archimedes is presumed to have shouted out at the Roman conqueror as he swung his blood-drenched sword above the scholar's head: "Noli tangere circulos meos!" ("Touch not my drawings!")

The face of the elderly man who portrayed himself in this drawing is familiar to many Leningraders: this sheet, which has come to symbolize the indomitable spirit of the creative ardour of the city's intellectuals during that time of trial, introduces a sketch-book on the title page of which the artist wrote in his own hand: "This is a collection of sketches and drawings made by Alexander Nikolsky in the Hermitage Air-raid Shelter No. 3, partly from life and partly from memory during the autumn and winter of 1941." Today this sketch-book is in the Hermitage Department of Prints and Drawings together with masterpieces executed by the world's greatest graphic artists. These drawings made by the architect Alexander Nikolsky during the long drawn-out nights of the siege are of priceless value for the Hermitage's war-time history.

When the war broke out many of the Hermitage's cellars were converted into air-raid shelters. As the carpenters and masons previously employed by the museum had all gone off to the front, the researchers themselves bricked up the basement windows, reinforced the doors with iron plating, knocked together crude sleeping benches and brought down tables and chairs. In the autumn and winter of 1941 these shelters afforded refuge to some two thousand people, including not only the Hermitage staff and their families but also many noted people in the worlds of science and the arts. There were twelve of these shelters which offered fairly reliable protection to their occupants at night when shells and bombs burst in the black skies overhead that were crisscrossed by the probing beams of searchlights.

139

At the end of the first week of the war the marble statue of Voltaire was evacuated.

A lorry at the Hermitage entrance in Khalturin Street

140

Jean-Antoine Houdon. 1741–1828. France
Statue of Voltaire

141

*Only three canvases, three great paintings,
were packed together with their golden frames.*

Leonardo da Vinci. 1452–1519. Italy
Madonna and Child (The Litta Madonna)

142

*Every picture had its definite place
in the evacuation pattern.*

Photograph of 1941

Air-raid Shelter No. 3, in which the architect Alexander Nikolsky lived with other members of the Hermitage Museum staff, was in one of the cellars of the New Hermitage. To reach it, one had to pass through the immense Hall of Twenty Columns and several more museum rooms, come into the inner courtyard through one of the emergency exits, enter an archway and then descend the steps into the shelter.

"At night this route, from the doors of the Hermitage through its halls and passageways to the shelter itself was fantastic to the point of terror," Alexander Nikolsky noted in his siege diary. "The enormous museum windows were not blacked out and of course no lamps could be lit, except for the tiny guide bulbs on the floor at each end of the Hall of Twenty Columns that were fed by the storage batteries standing there. Everything around was as black as soot. All that twinkled up ahead in the inky darkness was the tiny guide lamp."

Elsewhere in his siege diary Alexander Nikolsky wrote: "After moving into Air-raid Shelter No. 1 I began to sketch extensively... in October I sketched air-raid shelters from life, in November, the Neva with its ships from memory, and in December, the halls, rooms and passageways of the Hermitage itself."

Alexander Nikolsky staged his first showing of siege sketches right there in Air-raid Shelter No. 3. One day or night in December he invited his neighbours of the Hermitage staff and friends and acquaintances living in the other Hermitage cellars to visit him in his corner of the shelter where he had spread the selected sketches on the table, in front of which he drew up an armchair. With the words "Let me show you my drawings," he sat down on a stool by the armchair.

143

Leonardo da Vinci. 1452–1519. Italy
Madonna with a Flower (The Benois Madonna)

144

Raphael. 1483–1520. Italy
Madonna and Child (The Conestabile Madonna)

Crowding about in tightly belted quilted jackets, and muffled in woollen scarves and shawls, were Nikolsky's comrades, who, before the war, had frequented all art exhibitions both in Leningrad and Moscow. In the flickering light of the candles that cast fanciful shadows on the vaulted ceiling and walls of the cellar, on the cold flagstone floor and on the bed sheets hung between the cots and benches, Alexander Nikolsky once again said: "I will now show you my drawings."

As the first sheet was placed on the rests of the armchair, all saw a sketch of the air-raid shelter to which they had now come, with its cots and sleeping

145

The Hermitage treasures, prepared for the third evacuation train, remained in the Rastrelli Gallery.

War-time photograph

146, 147

The Rastrelli Gallery in the Winter Palace Designed by Bartolommeo Francesco Rastrelli. 1753–59

benches with the suspended bed sheets between them, the tables piled with books, and the figures of people muffled up in scarves and shawls. Next came a sketch depicting Air-raid Shelter No. 2, a narrow corridor with a cylindrical vault buttressed by trusses, then a drawing of Air-raid Shelter No. 5, the most dependable of all, which was beneath the rooms hitherto devoted to Egyptian art, and then again the drawing of another air-raid shelter, this time No. 7, which lay beneath the side nave of the rooms that had been given over before to Italian art, and which were "embellished," if one may employ that epithet, by a countless number of pipes snaking along the ceiling, which, now dead and no longer radiating warmth, had hitherto served as conduits for the warm air pumped through them.

As sheet alternated with sheet on the armchair rests, one saw the Neva as seen from a Hermitage window, again an air-raid shelter, the gloomy fronts of the Hermitage buildings, the depressing interiors of the Hermitage rooms and halls, stripped and denuded of all their former glory.

145

"That's all," Nikolsky said as he put the last sheet back on the table. Subsequently he asked a bookbinder on the Hermitage staff to make a large folder for the sketches he had drawn, and when that had been done, he drew the title-page: "This is a collection of sketches and drawings made by Alexander Nikolsky in the Hermitage Air-raid Shelter No. 3..."

Nikolsky stacked the heavy folder with the siege sketches alongside the wall where there were other folders holding the sketches, studies and blueprints which he continued to work at, even though the war had intervened, interrupting the construction of a stadium he had designed, and which, he was absolutely convinced, would be resumed after the victory; and of the vast seaside park, which he was certain would be laid out around the stadium after the war. With an itch for work that he simply could not resist, he would pick up a pencil with his numbed fingers and there would emerge, on the rough paper he was forced to use, the Triumphal Arch that would definitely be erected after the war to honour the victorious Soviet troops.

The fire-spotters now wrapped themselves in sheepskins when they needed to climb up onto the snow-laden roof of the Winter Palace —

which, incidentally, had not been cleared ever since the first snowfall. No wonder, as a biting, icy wind swirled freely there raking up snow that stung frozen faces.

At first a solitary Heinckel appeared in the skies overhead. The whining drone of its engines could be heard from quite some distance away. It dropped a parachute flare, and the fire-spotters and the ARP wardens posted above the Armorial Hall and near the skylights of the New Hermitage would always think each time that that accursed Heinckel had placed the flare right above the Hermitage and that the very first Nazi bomber wave would rain all its devastating cargo right down upon this brightly illumined roof.

True enough, Junkers bombers were already roaring overhead. The bombs burst on the Neva River churning up the ice and causing fountains of black spray to spatter the embankment. The walls of the palaces shuddered and despite the tremendous thunder of the explosions the attuned

ears of the spotters caught the tinkle of shattered glass as the blasts from the detonating bombs crashed through the window panes.

The third month of the Leningrad siege was about to end. An ice-cold December was raging.

Tikhvin had fallen to the enemy only a month earlier. The war had unexpectedly transformed this small town, tucked away in the midst of woods and located outside the line of encirclement, into a major railway hub. It was via Tikhvin that freight was delivered to the wharves and jetties on the eastern shores of Lake Ladoga, from where they were ferried across

150

*The evacuation campaign was over,
our life on roofs began!*

Photograph of 1941 (June)

151

*Sparks and soot rained down on the Hermitage
roof as the huge wooden structure of the roller
coaster was burning down on the opposite
bank of the Neva.*

The roller coaster on fire
Drawing by Alexander Nikolsky. 1941

to the other side, despite the deluge of bombs that they had to dodge. This was the one and only waterway that still linked Leningrad with the mainland. Tikhvin was captured by the enemy on November 8, and on that day, in order to stretch out Leningrad's already meagre store of provisions, the bread ration was reduced even for the troops in the front line. It was cut once again less than a week later, on November 13; now factory workers got a daily ration of three hundred grammes, while all others, even children under twelve years of age, received half that amount. Barely another week had passed, when the bread ration was again cut, now to a mere two hundred and fifty grammes for factory workers, and to half that amount for all others. One must realize that then bread was virtually the sole food! Death was ready to strangle people by the thousands with the bony hand of hunger.

Snowswept streets and avenues. Houses garbed in hoarfrost inside and out. Windows in which not a solitary light twinkled. They were blacked out, if not boarded up, and whether there might be behind them the flickering flame of a wick that smoked and sputtered, as it floated in a saucer or pot of some combustible or other, was anyone's guess. Still the famous siege wick was a flame that never dimmed. In its flicker poets composed army leaflets and artists drew army posters for the fighting front. It also illumined the engineer's drawing board and the scholar's desk.

For a long while the Hermitage managed to dispense with this makeshift light. By some fluke its stores produced a generous quantity of church candles, while in some rooms electric lights even burned, all thanks to the navy.

It so happened that in early winter, when the Hermitage had all electricity supplies cut off for reasons that were noted earlier, A. Tripolsky, a famous submarine commander, came to the Hermitage. He was a well-known personality there as his portrait had been displayed in the Hermitage

152–154

The paintings of the Raphael Loggias were not taken away from the Hermitage: it seemed to be too risky an affair to remove the canvases from the walls and vaults. The thirteen windows of the old gallery were carefully boarded up with thick planking and sand-bagged.

The Raphael Loggias
Designed by Giacomo Quarenghi. 1783–92

gallery of Heroes of the Soviet Union. He peeped into one of the rooms, then into another and each time caught a glimpse of elderly folk, wrapped in heavy overcoats with the collars pulled up to their ears to guard against the icy cold, writing at their desks.

In the Director's study the desk was likewise piled high with books and manuscripts. Orbeli greeted his visitor warmly: after all he never forgot that Tripolsky's submariners had also contributed to the effort to evacuate the Hermitage treasures. Dusk was falling, and removing the plaid blanket he had drawn across his lap and knees to help him somewhat alleviate the rheumatic pains that "are simply tormenting me," as he confessed to the naval officer, Orbeli rose from his chair and having set up a candle, was about to black out the window, when, having second thoughts, suggested: "Let's better go downstairs. It's a bit warmer there."

In the Hall of Twenty Columns, through which they had to pass, it was pitch dark. The storage batteries that had fed the guide lights had run down completely. Now the only guide in the darkness was a church candle that flickered on the floor by the door in the opposite wall. Orbeli marched along in front and whenever he blocked the view of the twinkling glow on the floor in the distance, Tripolsky was obliged to grope his way forward, stretching out a hand to touch the cold stone of each column.

In the next hall, the glow from another candle, also placed on the floor, was reflected in the shiny jasper of the famous Kolyvan Vase, a nineteen-ton piece that is two and a half metres high, five metres across at the lip and three metres across at the base.

Emerging into an inner courtyard thanks to this guiding light, they followed a beaten pathway through the snow, under an archway. Here a flight of steps led down into the cellars, where to the right was the entrance to Air-raid Shelter No. 3 and opposite it, to the left, the door to Orbeli's room.

The fetid smell of dampness pervaded the air. Striking a match, Iosif Orbeli lit a candle in a three-branch candlestick.

"My blockade office," he smiled, letting his bushy beard straggle out over his quilted jacket from the warm scarf in which he had muffled it before. A vaulted ceiling, a narrow cot by the wall, and books, seemingly scores of them, strewn on the floor.

Tripolsky could not tear his eyes away from the sputtering candle. Thinking that his visitor was interested in this heavily chased silver candlestick, Orbeli began to speak enthusiastically of the medieval silversmiths who had crafted it. Tripolsky listened, nodding from time to time, but his thoughts were preoccupied with other matters.

Stepping out of the main entrance of the Hermitage, he crossed over to the parapet of the embankment. Ranged nearby was the ice-blocked *Poliarnaya Zvezda* (*Pole Star*), the former pleasure yacht of the imperial family, and now an auxiliary vessel for the submarine squadron that he

155

As travelling to the Urals might become fatal to
the five-hundred-year-old fresco, it was left on the wall,
with a breastwork of sand put up as a temporary defence.

Fra Giovanni da Fiesole. *C.* 1400–1455. Italy
Madonna and Child with St Dominic and St Thomas Aquinas

156, 157

*The marble statues of Roman emperors
stand round the statue of Jupiter,
the biggest in the Hermitage, almost three
and a half metres tall.*

The Jupiter Hall in the New Hermitage
Built by Vasily Stasov and Nikolai Yefimov
after Leo von Klenze's design. 1842–51

158

Head of a Syrian Woman
Rome. 150–175 A.D.

159

Portrait of Philip the Arabian
Rome. 3rd century A.D.

160

Marble sarcophagus
Rome. Late 2nd century A.D.

156

158

159

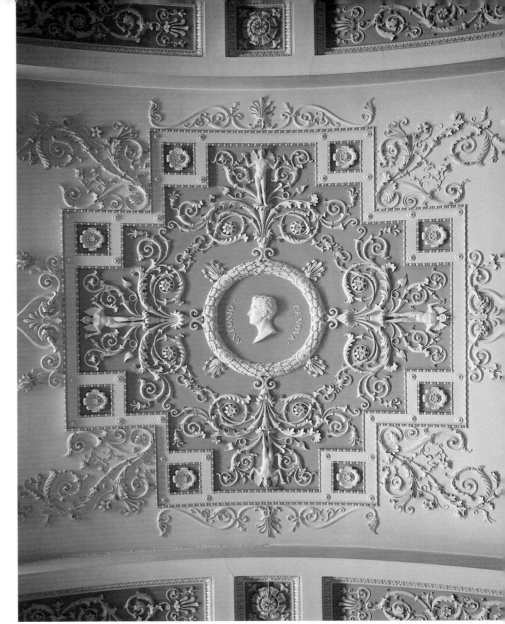

157

160

161

161

Boxes with objects of semi-precious stones stand at the pedestal of the sixteen-ton statue of Jupiter.

The Jupiter Hall during the siege

162

Quartz vase
Ekaterinburg Lapidary Factory
Russia. 19th century

163

Marble vase
Italy. Late 18th century

commanded. Tripolsky climbed aboard up the slippery gangway and at once descended into the engine room to talk with the electricians. The next morning sailors laid a cable across the road to the Hermitage. "The ship fed electricity to several of the Hermitage rooms," the architect Alexander Nikolsky noted in his siege diary. "It was light now where it had been dark before and this was of priceless worth."

However, the yacht could not share much electricity. What the Hermitage got was only enough to light a few rooms; elsewhere candles continued to burn on desks and tables, and in their glow, papers rustled as numbed fingers leafed through unfinished manuscripts. Piotrovsky, the Hermitage Museum's present Director, recalled later: "Our scholarly exercises greatly eased our hardships, as those who had something to occupy their minds with throughout the day more easily bore the pangs

of hunger. With the passage of time the sense of hunger developed into a physical morbidity unlike that ordinary feeling of hunger which a person may experience in ordinary times. But like any indisposition it is easier to withstand when one is engaged in some activity."

Meanwhile, outside, bombs and shells continued to explode, now near by, now further away. The tallow candles sputtered, while the history of the culture of ancient Urartu assumed more and more distinctive form on paper under the pen of Boris Piotrovsky, now the deputy chief of the fire wardens.

From the slopes of Karmir Blur in far-away Armenia Boris Piotrovsky had returned to Leningrad to take up arms and fight for the city he loved so dearly. However, that was not to be. He was ordered by the military command to stay on at the Hermitage and take part in the defence work. That term embraced a wide range of concerns. It was necessary to safeguard everything at the Hermitage that had not been evacuated. It was necessary likewise to protect the Academy of Sciences collection, which had been deposited with the Hermitage after the siege began. It was necessary in near-frontline conditions and despite the daily bombardment and shelling to preserve the buildings of the Hermitage as historic and artistic monuments of priceless value, as gems that were the creations of great architects. Recruited from the museum staff was a "crash rescue team" for emergency restoration work. They, as archival documents say, "speedily and with surprising dexterity and skill undertook to make good the breakdowns and damage caused to the buildings

by the shelling and bombardment." The fire-fighting team, recruited mainly from among the Hermitage Museum researchers, also did a fine job, contributing significantly to the saving of its buildings.

Note that even earlier, in peace time — and also after the war — the Hermitage was on the priority list of the city's fire brigade. As soon as the war broke out the number of fire-warden posts at the Hermitage was greatly increased, and manned, the moment the air-raid alert was sounded, by local ARP wardens. "During the autumn and winter of 1941–42 there used to be as many as ten to twelve air-raid alerts sounded daily," Boris Piotrovsky recalled later.

166

165

164

The huge Kolyvan vase (two and a half metres tall and four and a half metres in diameter, weighing nineteen tons) is a unique example of Russian stone carving. During the siege water which accumulated in it was bailed out.

Vase of Revniovo jasper (The Kolyvan Vase)
Russia. 19th century

165

Mediaeval arms and armour lay during the siege on the mosaic floor of the Hall of the Swan.

The Hall of the Swan in the New Hermitage
Built by Vasily Stasov and Nikolai Yefimov
after Leo von Klenze's design. 1842–51

166

Partisan. Germany. 1614
Fauchard. Italy. Late 16th – early 17th century

167

*Porcelain figurines lay on a thick layer of sand
on the stone floor of the cellar.*

Faience ware. Germany. 19th century

168

One of the rooms of antique art
in the New Hermitage after the artillery
shelling

169

The porcelain which had not been evacuated was stored under this hall in the cellar.

The Athena Hall in the New Hermitage Built by Vasily Stasov and Nikolai Yefimov after Leo von Klenze's design. 1842–51

"At night we were obliged to run to our posts through the pitch-dark rooms and halls of the Hermitage and Winter Palace. However, we grew so used to these routes, which at times were as much as three quarters of a kilometre long, that we could have done it blindfolded."

"It was extremely cold in the halls and rooms," he continued. "On my tours of inspection I used to bring to my colleagues, manning the posts, mugs of what we called tea, but which was actually no more than tepid water, unsweetened and, of course, without any tea in it at all. Still, though I passed through the palace halls and rooms time and time again both during the day and at night, I simply could not accustom the eye to their forlorn character — even though now, bare and empty, their splendid architecture and decoration was brought home with particular force. At night they

would be illumined by the glare of nearby fires or the dazzle of incendiary bombs which were fizzling out in the vicinity."

The moment the "all clear" was sounded, Piotrovsky went back to his room, to his beloved Urartu, and filled page after page with his neat handwriting. Now and again he would jot down in the margin the words "terribly cold" or "it's hard to write, it's so cold."

It was, indeed, terribly cold and one was infernally hungry. Two hundred and fifty grammes of adulterated bread for a factory worker on his ration book, and only half that amount for the office employee did not suffice. In such conditions a jelly of joiner's glue was truly a feast for the gods. Eve-of-the-war plans had called for extensive repairs at the Hermitage and goodly stocks of joiner's glue and drying oil had been laid in. At times just half a kilo of joiner's glue plus a litre of natural drying oil

170–177 Sheets from Alexander Nikolsky's sketch-book. Winter of 1941–42

170

At night the route to the Hermitage air-raid shelters was fantastic to the point of terror.

could save a life. As was said, joiner's glue was boiled down into a kind of jelly, while the drying oil was employed to fry "fritters" made of the peelings of frozen spuds that somebody had somehow managed to rake up.

With the fire-fighting wardens in their quarters all talk of food was taboo. There was a stove there that went at full blast and lamps burned thanks to the electricity fed by cable from the *Pole Star* yacht. It was not only the fire wardens that came round to warm up; often Iosif Orbeli himself or other members of the museum staff would come up there from the air-raid shelters. "The fire wardens' room became the pivot of academic life at the Hermitage," Boris Piotrovsky noted in his siege diary. As a matter of fact it was in that room that the suggestion was made to mark the five hundredth anniversary of the great Uzbek poet Alisher Navoi, the lengthy preparations for which had been interrupted at the Hermitage by the outbreak of war.

Incidentally, that was the second highlight in the world of literature to be celebrated, if one can really say that, at the Hermitage Museum in the besieged Leningrad. The first came earlier in October 1941 and was dedicated to the eight hundredth anniversary of the great Azerbaijanian thinker and poet Nizami of Gianja.

When Orbeli first put forward his plan for celebrating the Nizami jubilee, the Leningrad Front Command told him outright that his project was unrealistic, to say the least. "Suppose you have an enemy air raid right at that very moment? Who will guarantee the safety of all the city's most prominent intellectuals who will have gathered for the event?" But Orbeli was adamant. "I'll guarantee their safety," he insisted. "After all, the first bomb will certainly not score a direct hit, I'm sure of that, and by the time a second one comes down I'll have all of them safe and sound inside the air-raid shelter!"

Eventually the Nizami jubilee was marked; the celebration started at two in the afternoon and closed just a mere two minutes before the air-raid alert was sounded. Curiously enough Orbeli was informed about a week later that because of the war the Nizami eight hundredth anniversary celebrations that had been scheduled in many places, including Moscow and Baku, the capital of the Soviet Caucasian republic of Azerbaijan, had been called off, which meant that the only place where the event had been marked was the besieged Leningrad.

Again Orbeli had to use his eloquence to persuade the Leningrad Front Command to give permission for marking the Navoi jubilee, scheduled for December, noting how significant it was and what a memorable occasion this would be. He succeeded. He even managed to get them to release from frontline duties a number of Orientalists and poets who before the war had translated Navoi's verses into Russian.

As on the eve of the event another eight tram lines had ceased functioning due to the electricity shortage—as a matter of fact, that meant that virtually no more trams would be running—the soldier-poets and the soldier-Orientalists, whom their commanding officers had allowed to attend the celebrations at the Hermitage, were forced to go on foot along the winding footpaths that took them past the tall snowdrifts and the snowswept trams frozen on the snowswept tracks.

Both the Palace Embankment and the bridge spanning the Winter Canal were waist-deep in snow. However, the Small Entrance, the one by which

171, 174

*In the autumn and winter of 1941 two thousand
people — museum workers and art scholars —
lived in the twelve air-raid shelters of the Hermitage.*

171

173

174

172

172

New Year tree in one of the Hermitage air-raid shelters

173

Entrance to Air-raid Shelter No. 3; on the left, the door to Orbeli's study

175, 176

In the morning, some of the air-raid shelter dwellers went to the Hermitage rooms, others to the Academy of Arts, still others to make sketches in the streets of the besieged Leningrad.

museum staff entered the museum, had been cleared of snow and inside, behind the door, Academician Orbeli himself stood welcoming guests to the Navoi festival. He was especially happy to see them on that day, the day when they had to make tremendous efforts to come from their frost-trimmed apartments, which now seemed so far away, and from the frontline dugouts which, with the enemy tightening its grip around the encircled city, were now ever closer.

The celebration took place in the so-called School Room, where before the war the Hermitage Museum's teenage enthusiasts had attended lectures and seminars, a spacious room but now a bleak and cold place where the staff meetings were held. Iosif Orbeli, the chairman, took off his overcoat, and, remaining in his warm muffler and padded jacket, declared: "We have gathered here under incredible circumstances and at a most

139

unusual time, which our city and our entire Soviet land are going through, to observe a most remarkable highlight in the life of the Soviet peoples — to render tribute to the immortal name of the great poet and enlightener Alisher Navoi. This very fact alone of our paying homage to the poet's memory in beleaguered Leningrad, ordained to suffer from hunger and the cold, in a city that the enemy believes dead and drained of blood, only once again demonstrates our people's stalwart spirit, their defiant resolve and will and the eternally living humane heart of Soviet science..."

177

Every evening, returning to Air-raid Shelter No. 3, Alexander Nikolsky passed through the pitch-dark Hall of Twenty Columns with a tiny glimmering light showing the exit into the yard.

178

Oil-lamp
Drawing from Alexander Nikolsky's diary

At that moment a massive thump, which made the air tremble and the panes tinkle, was heard, as it seemed, from quite close at hand, and all rushed to the large windows. There followed almost at once a second thud and a water spout rose up from the Neva, scattering spray in every direction.

"Don't be alarmed, comrades," Orbeli said calmly, suggesting that the audience perhaps retire to the air-raid shelter. However, everybody sat down again and Orbeli continued: "Very well, we shall proceed."

Every conceivable misfortune and calamity that the historians of old had chronicled in accounts of famous sieges of impregnable fortresses and citadels starved into surrender and then laid waste by fire and sword, every conceivable instrument and weapon of destruction and death that could be culled from the darkness of history and that were multiplied by such sophisticated and supermodern means of annihilation as long-range artillery and bomber aircraft, in short, everything conceivable and inconceivable was employed by the Nazis to batter down Russia's glorious, legendary city of Leningrad. However, this metropolis, which so proudly bears the great name of Lenin, staunchly defied the enemy, its gallant defenders displaying miracles of heroism in the field

179, 180

The mosaic floor and ceiling painting were plunged in darkness.

The Hall of Twenty Columns.
Floor and ceiling

and its citizens a moral fortitude of unexampled power and might. While artillery shells and bombs transformed houses, factories and palaces into heaps of rubble, in the murky gloom of an air-raid shelter in the Hermitage cellars, a Russian architect had a vision of those majestic edifices that he would erect after victory was won. And while hunger stalked the encircled city and the cold froze to the marrow its starving citizens, in the Hermitage School Room its emaciated, gaunt and weary scholars and researchers forgot the gnawing pangs of hunger and the numbing iciness as they presented and listened to papers concerned with the life and work of the great Uzbek poet Alisher Navoi, who had been active in the fifteenth century in faraway Central Asia.

"This was no plain and simple self-complacent resignation, no escapism, no withdrawal into the seclusion of the monastic cell," Piotrovsky

181–183

*During the hardest days of the war, during the most difficult
days of the siege the architect Alexander Nikolsky, believing
in the inevitable victory of the Soviet people, was designing
triumphal arches in honour of the victorious Soviet Army.*

Sheets from Alexander Nikolsky's sketch-book.
Winter of 1941–42

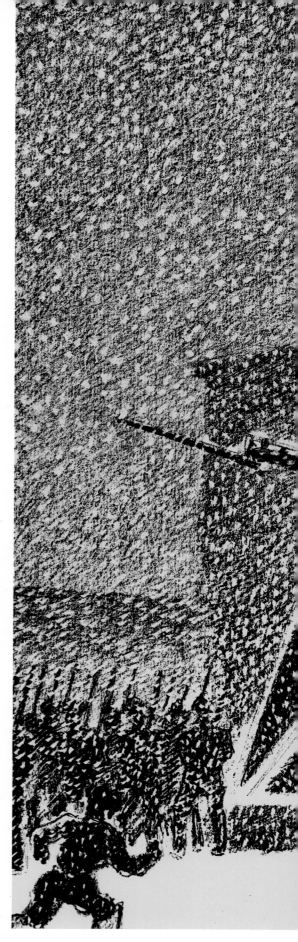

wrote, commenting on the Navoi jubilee in one of the Hermitage war-time propaganda leaflets. "Rather this work was concerned with the study of the culture of the peoples of the Soviet Union, welded together into one, united, fraternal family of nations capable of promoting and advancing this culture, a family of nations that no technical means whatever in the hands of the enemies of our Motherland will ever serve to vanquish and enslave."

During the three days the Navoi festival continued, Orbeli had no time to make his customary daily inspection of the Hermitage rooms and halls. And, believe it or not, in all these three days he did not feel the afflictions of rheumatism once. It seemed as if the disease had condescendingly granted him a respite. However, the moment the session was over, it attacked again, and though his legs, indeed every joint, ached, he did not allow himself to forego his daily round of inspection, which he usually commenced on the second floor, it being easier to go on foot down rather than up.

As he passed from room to room, the wall mirrors reflected the invariable navy-blue quilted jacket in which his stooped figure was garbed, the black fur cap, the windows that had been boarded up with plywood and the hoarfrost riming the walls. He stretched out a hand to touch the wall — it was ice-cold. It seemed to him as if the denuded picture frames on the frosted walls breathed the December wintriness. Thoughts veered to the faraway town of Sverdlovsk in the Urals and there seemed to appear before his eyes a vision of the three buildings specially assigned to house the evacuated treasures of the Hermitage, so graphically described in letters received: namely the local picture gallery, the building of a former Catholic church and the Museum of Atheism, which were crammed ceiling high with all the crates and boxes despatched from Leningrad. How were matters faring there in Sverdlovsk, he wondered. The mail was now highly irregular. But what a grand consolation it was to learn that at the walls of Moscow Hitler's armies had been put to rout and were forced to retreat, which, perchance, signalled a turn in the tides of the war: and also that the little town of Tikhvin had been retaken.

In the state rooms of the Winter Palace, so enormous now that they were stripped of their furnishings and echoing back the slightest footstep, it was still chillier than in the New Hermitage. Thus far enemy bombs had spared both the Winter Palace and the Hermitage. True, a high-explosive bomb had exploded in the courtyard of the Hermitage Theatre, but the buildings of both palace and museum were thus far intact, except for the pockmarks left on the front by the flying splinters and the broken window panes shattered by the blasts.

He paused at a boarded-up window. It appeared that the plywood had warped and that some amount of snow had drifted in through the crack onto the sill. More snow had slipped down onto the parquet floor, which was still strewn with slivers of shattered panes. Evidently, when going through the hall at night, someone had stepped right into the heap of sand by the doorway and had unintentionally spread the sand all over the floor; it crunched underfoot, as nobody had yet swept it away. Again he would have to rebuke someone for having failed to do this chore. But could he really do that now that these starving people had reached their last tether, and yet were doing all that was humanly possible in those circumstances? Tikhvin had been retaken, which might, perchance, somewhat ease Leningrad's desperate plight.

Orbeli next descended into the rooms that had formerly been given over to a display of the arts of Antiquity. He went through the rooms where the statues of Athena and Hercules stood and then turned back. There was nothing of the oppressive emptiness of the upstairs rooms here, as stacked up in the ground-floor rooms of the New Hermitage were the unevacuated objects that had formerly been exhibited in the rooms on the first and second floors.

In the Hall of the Swan, a room whose architecture had been specially designed to reproduce the inner patio characteristic of the palatial villas of Ancient Greece or Rome, piles of medieval arms and armour, sundry pikes, halberds, two-handled broadswords and cuirasses and coats of mail lay in confusion on the mosaic floor between the pedestals on which the evacuated ancient sculpture had once stood. In the hall where the colossal statue of Jupiter towered, he had to pick his way carefully along one of the two narrow pathways left between the masses of Western European engraved gems and objects made of semi-precious stones from the Urals that now cluttered the entire room from wall to wall.

Orbeli's tour of inspection ended where it had begun—in the vestibule of the service entrance. Here, on the steps, he saw a heap of rucksacks and bundles knotted with twine, which meant that members of the staff had again brought back for safekeeping to the Hermitage exhibits from the museum building in Solianoi Pereulok (Salt Lane). Established by the patron of arts Stieglitz beyond the Field of Mars at the close of the past century, in the 1920s it had been attached to the Hermitage as a branch. As due to the siege it had not been possible to evacuate its fine collections of objects of

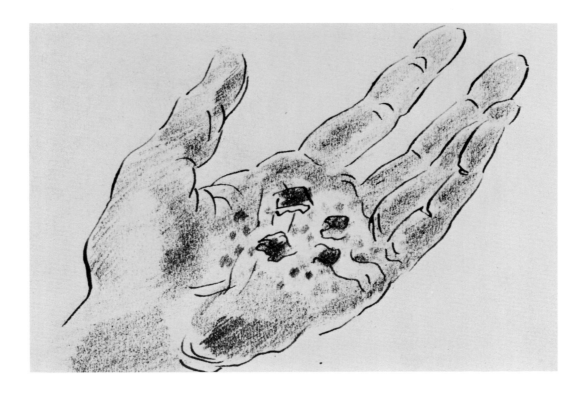

184
Daily bread ration
Drawing
from Alexander
Nikolsky's diary

the applied and decorative arts, it had been decided to remove them to the Hermitage in the autumn. It had so happened that one autumn day during an air raid, the chief warden on duty at the Hermitage had been informed over the phone that the Stieglitz building had received a direct hit. Iosif Orbeli tried phoning back but it was no use, the line was out of order. He rushed over to Salt Lane and was told that the bomb had destroyed some of the items, but that luckily nobody of the staff had been hurt. The place still reeked of cordite, the walls had cracked and in places the plaster had peeled off to reveal the brickwork beneath. The glass dome of the central hall had been blasted to smithereens and the light autumn drizzle came pattering down right through onto the parquet floor, strewn with slivers of glass, splinters of mahogany and shattered porcelain, all of which crunched underfoot.

At this point it would be appropriate to note that objects of art are still more susceptible to disease than a living organism. Exposed to the damp and the open air, some of the Salt Lane museum items were mouldy or corroded even before they could be removed from the partly demolished building. As no trucks or cars were available, Orbeli and his staff had to carry everything over to the Hermitage by handcart. However, when the winter snows began, the carts stalled in the drifts and so the Hermitage staff either used sleds, to which they harnessed themselves to transport the more massive objects, or carried the lighter items in rucksacks or simply in their hands or under an arm.

As Orbeli now looked at the pile of rucksacks and bundles on the steps in the vestibule of the service entrance, he thought to himself that now with Tikhvin retaken, things might ease somewhat and he would be able to get a lorry for the Hermitage needs.

It was the 29th of December. The year of 1941 was drawing to a close.

The fierce and furious artillery bombardment of the neighbourhood of Palace Square and the Winter Palace commenced around midday. One shell hit the southern wing of the Winter Palace near the Kitchen Yard. A second exploded in front of the side that faced on the Admiralty. A third hit the portico that the granite atlantes bore. Orbeli inspected the damage. The crushed brick stained the snow red like splotches of caked blood. The massive cornice had caved slightly inwards, intersected by a deeply furrowed crack. A fragment of granite had been shaved off one of the stone atlantes, scarring its glistening torso.

Orbeli's hopes were not fated to materialize. January 1942 displayed no mercy. The besieged city was cruelly ravaged by frosts that dropped to 30° C below zero. Ice and snow held undisputed sway over house, street and square; the deserted embankments merged with the Neva River beneath one solid sheet of hummock-studded ice. The battered buildings of the Hermitage and Winter Palace stared unseeingly at the ice-locked river with their blocked-up and boarded-over windows.

185

The Palace Embankment.
The Main Entrance to the Hermitage
War-time photograph

186

The Polar Star, *moored
at the Winter Canal,
fed the Hermitage rooms
with electricity.*

Drawing by Alexander Nikolsky

187

Frozen ships on the Neva as seen
from the Hermitage
Drawing by Alexander Nikolsky

188

*Day and night sentries stood
at the Hermitage entrances.*

War-time photograph

The frosts were savagely cruel and the ice on Lake Ladoga held strong beneath the Road of Life, and towards the close of January Leningrad radio announced an increase in bread rations. This was the second such increase, as still earlier, when shortly after the re-capture of Tikhvin, food deliveries to Leningrad had slightly improved, the Military Council of the Leningrad Front resolved to raise bread rations on December 25, 1941, adding a hundred grammes for factory workers and seventy-five grammes for all the rest. While a month later, as was said, towards the close of January 1942, when the roadways across the ice of Lake Ladoga were heavy with traffic, the bread ration was again raised to four hundred grammes per factory worker, to three hundred grammes for office employees and to two hundred and fifty grammes for children and dependants. A fortnight later, on the 11th of February, new bread rations went into force with five hundred grammes doled out to factory workers, four hundred grammes to office employees and three hundred grammes to all others.

However, the lethal hand of hunger that had started already in November to throttle the citizens of Leningrad refused to withdraw. People were so greatly emaciated by starvation and so greatly worn down by the cold

191

192

189

Vladimir Loewinson-Lessing headed the group of curators responsible for the evacuated museum collection.

Drawing by Georgy Vereysky. 1961

190

The Hermitage at night
Drawing by Georgy Vereysky. 1942

191

Orbeli: "I constantly thought of the Hermitage treasures despatched to the Urals."

Drawing by Georgy Vereysky. March, 1942

192

Mikhail Dobroklonsky, the Chief Curator of the Hermitage during the siege.

Drawing by Georgy Vereysky. 1939

that the death toll in the besieged Leningrad continued to soar — from 11,085 in November to 52,881 in December, and still more in January and February.

Nor were the Hermitage staff spared, though to the last hour they continued to board up shattered windows, clear away the snow from the parquet flooring in the rooms, and tirelessly fill sheet after sheet of manuscripts. But life ebbed and death gave no quarter.

Yet though people were on their last legs, though the mournful roll-call of the dead lengthened with every day, the Road of Life linking Leningrad with the mainland across the ice of Lake Ladoga continued to function. On that same day of January 24, when the announcement was broadcast that the bread ration in Leningrad was to be increased, the city authorities announced from Smolny — that historical, revolutionary and architectural highlight, which had once housed the college for the daughters of the nobility and was subsequently the seat, directly after the October Revolution, of the first Soviet Government — that a small convalescent centre was to be established at the Hermitage. According to the plan it was to take in staff not only from the Hermitage but also from another four of the city's museums; however, the Hermitage people were to be placed in charge and were to run the entire affair. It took but one short week to get ready a total of one

193

Those who were invited to attend the Nizami Festival went to the Small Entrance — the service entrance to the Hermitage.

At the Small Entrance
Sheet from Alexander Nikolsky's sketch-book. Winter of 1941—42

194

195   196

hundred cots that were set up on the ground floor of de La Mothe's Pavilion. Further, several ladies from amongst the Hermitage keepers and curators were appointed to tend to the sick.

Hospitalization in the Hermitage convalescent centre—which was closed down only on May 1, 1942—saved many a life; yet, on the other hand no small number were so emaciated that neither the increased ration nor intravenous shots of glucose could save them from death.

By February the Hermitage air-raid shelters became empty. The electricity and heating had gone off in 1941, while in January 1942 the water and sewage pipes froze. Whereas earlier the war-weary people had found at least refuge from the shelling and bombing

1141—1941

Государственный Эрмитаж приглашает Вас на

ТОРЖЕСТВЕННОЕ ЗАСЕДАНИЕ

посвященное 800-летию со дня рождения великого Азербайджанского поэта

НИЗАМИ ГАНДЖЕВИ

Заседание состоится **19** октября 1941 г. в **14** часов, вход с Малого подъезда, Набережная 9 Января, 34

При входе в Эрмитаж обязательно предъявление документов и настоящего билета

М 81726   2-я типо-лит. Гидрометеоиздата, з. 2178 - 600

198

"The State Hermitage invites you to the celebration devoted to the 800th anniversary of the great Azerbaijanian poet Nizami of Gianja..."

An invitation card to the Nizami Festival in the Hermitage on October 19, 1941

199
The Tent Hall during the siege

200

201

200

Pieter Claesz. 1597–1661
Holland
Pipes in a Brazier

201

Jan Huysum. 1682–1740
Holland
Flowers

202

Willem Claesz Heda.
1594 – between 1680 and 1682
Holland
Still Life with Lobster

203, 204

The Tent Hall in the New Hermitage
Built by Vasily Stasov and Nikolai Yefimov
after Leo von Klenze's design. 1842–51

203

within these vaulted cellars, now, with practically every Leningrader accustomed to the shelling and the bombing, they had to contend here with the cold, the darkness and the miasma of decay. In short, there came the day when the living were gone and only the dead were left in the air-raid shelters.

Orbeli moved up from the shelter to a small room right above the service entrance and it was here that he was obliged to enter into rather embarrassing conversations with members of the staff in February and March. The point was that as soon as the Road of Life started functioning across the ice-bound Lake Ladoga, the State Committee of Defence in Moscow resolved to evacuate from Leningrad some half a million of its inhabitants. Orbeli's job was to try to persuade as many of his staff as he could to evacuate from the besieged city. He indulged in lengthy explanations to convince each of them that the wholesale evacuation was of crucial significance for the country, that it would ease the defence effort in the city, and that, as far as the Hermitage was concerned, it would save the lives of many scholars of great worth. Moreover, there were plans to "mothball" museums, including the Hermitage, which would entail staff reductions. He was heard out, after which staff members trooped in one after another to put on his desk statements that were practically as similar as two peas. "Can't leave Leningrad," "do not wish to go" or "have no desire to evacuate," was written on almost each page before him. "I adore the Hermitage and would be only too happy to work and contribute the best I can, whatever I may be asked to do." The list of the people from the Hermitage Museum staff who heeded Iosif Orbeli's persuasive advice was short indeed. Yet what could he tell all those who were so adamant in their decision to stay in Leningrad? Had he himself not spent the entire winter attempting to get permission to stay on in Leningrad? Had not he himself cited persuasive arguments to demonstrate that his job of preserving the Hermitage's treasures was still not fully done? Had not he himself rejected out of hand the point made that he was seriously ill, and had he not insisted that he felt far better than he had before the war? Indeed, even now, when all his powers of persuasion to allow him to stay on had failed, had not he himself so eloquently demanded and obtained at least a postponement until the work of "mothballing" the Hermitage was completed? But with his own staff he simply could not find the words to convince them that it was essential for them to evacuate.

Placing to one side the pile of refusals, he noted how many people he should retain on the staff while the Hermitage was mothballed. He wondered whom to appoint as keepers and curators, whom to employ as guards, and whom to use as handymen. Having perused once again the statements from all the members of the staff who had so firmly and categorically resolved to stay on, he drew up a report for Leningrad's mayor. The first man he thought of as adequate to substitute for him while he was away and to assume the duties of Director was Professor Mikhail Dobroklonsky, an eminent authority on Western European graphic art.

Although during the first three months of 1942 there was no aerial bombardment, the shelling from long-range guns continued. True, in January it abated a little, as now the German general Küchler,

whom Hitler had appointed commander in place of the dismissed Field Marshal von Leeb, had concentrated on disrupting supplies brought in to Leningrad across the Road of Life. Thus, in January the number of shells — 2,696 — fired at Leningrad was half the number fired in December. However, realizing that attempts to strangle Leningrad by starving its citizens had proved ineffective, he reverted to the previous strategy of systematically reducing the besieged city to rubble and ruin by gunfire. Thus, throughout February, the shortest month of the year, a total of 4,776 shells

205

Antonio Rossetti.
1819 – late 19th century. Italy
Esmeralda

206

*After one of the air-raids the Chief Curator
Mikhail Dobroklonsky saw a headless statue
of Esmeralda: evidently the blast wave smashed
the window pane and knocked off the head of the
statue; it lay on the parquet floor among the bits
of wood and shattered glass.*

Mikhail Dobroklonsky during his routine
inspection tour of the Hermitage

exploded within the city, while throughout the following month of March the
total was much higher, 7,380. The fire returned by Soviet long-range artillery by land and sea and Soviet bombing attacks forced the enemy to desist for a while; however, after two or three days of complete or partial lulls,
the shelling was resumed in full intensity with between two and three hundred shells fired at the city daily.

In January, March and April enemy shelling ravaged the buildings of the
Hermitage Museum. The crash rescue team repaired the damaged roofing,

and blocked up the shattered windows with plywood sheeting. The damage done to the Hermitage Museum was especially heavy on March 18, when six shells exploded right in the grounds of the Winter Palace. A large-calibre shell hit one of the walls facing the Kitchen Yard. It smashed right into a window jamb and destroyed part of the wall of the now empty depository of the Department of Prehistoric Culture. The blast completely shattered three thousand window panes, including the enormous windows on the second and third flights of the Main Staircase of the Winter Palace. This broad marble staircase was known in the eighteenth century as the Ambassadors' Staircase

209

Intaglio: *Mars and Bellona*
England. By Charles Brown. 1749–1795

210

The Gold Drawing-room in the Winter Palace
during the war

211

The Green Dining-room in the Winter Palace
Designed by Alexander Briullov. 1860s

212

Intaglio: *Daedalus and Icarus*
Italy. By Giovanni Bernardi di Castelbolognese.
Active in the 16th century

213

Intaglio: *Hercules and Antaeus*
Germany. By Ludwig Krug. 1488/90–1532

209

210

because foreign envoys used it to reach the state rooms of the Imperial Palace, and later it was renamed the Main Staircase as soon as the principal entrance to the rooms and exhibitions of the State Hermitage Museum was
opened to the public in Soviet times. All its flights, indeed every single step
is well lit by the daylight pouring in through the two tiers of high windows.
On March 18, all their panes were blown inwards by the blast of the exploding shell that hit the adjacent wall. The steps of the Main Staircase were
strewn with hundreds of slivers of broken glass. Meanwhile eddies of damp
snow, blown in by the March wind, now whirled past the marble walls and
in and out of the granite columns and the statues of the muses and deities
beneath the deep azure vault of sky of the ceiling panel that depicts Olympus bathed in glorious sunshine.

The broken glass still crunched underfoot when on March 30, Orbeli
ascended the Main Staircase on his last tour of inspection as Director before evacuating from Leningrad. As he made the round he bid farewell to

166

211

217

218

214

The Gold Drawing-room
in the Winter Palace
Drawing by Vera Miliutina. 1942

215

The Gold Drawing-room
in the Winter Palace
Designed by Vladimir
Schreiber (?). 1850s

216

Western European cameos
15th–17th centuries

217

*The Nazi troops are only
fourteen kilometres from Palace
Square, the Winter Palace,
and the Hermitage.*

View of Palace Square from
the Winter Palace
War-time photograph

218

The Cameo Room
Watercolour by Edward Hau.
1854

215

216

219, 220

222

219, 220

The Hall of Italian Majolica in the New Hermitage
Built by Vasily Stasov and Nikolai Yefimov
after Leo von Klenze's design. 1842–51

221

Italian majolica

222

The Hall of Italian Majolica during
the siege of Leningrad

friends and staff. He parted with the living. The dead still lay in the mortuary occupying the cellar beneath the Hermitage Library.

The burial squad came to the Hermitage in early April. They hoisted forty-six frozen corpses into the lorry that pulled up in the courtyard outside the mortuary. The corpses were taken off to a plot of wasteland on the city's outskirts, near the railway station of Piskariovka. The entire winter was spent digging deep trenches in the frozen ground and having trucks bring out from all over Leningrad the frozen corpses of men, women and children who had starved to death or who had been killed during the shelling or bombardment of the city. The common graves that were dug here on what was once the fringe of the city were subsequently transformed into the Piskariovskoye Memorial Cemetery, where the grief felt at the losses that Leningrad sustained during the war has been memorialized by granite and marble. Beneath the stones of the nameless graves of the Piskariovskoye Memorial Cemetery, where the Eternal Flame burns in commemoration of the dead, lie the remains of many who had once been on the Hermitage staff. Some were young, budding scholars, others were researchers of world repute, some were the elderly ladies from among the room attendants, others were joiners and electricians. Incised in the granite are the words: "Nobody is forgotten, nothing is forgotten."

223

Palace Square on October 14, 1942
Drawing by Nikolai Pavlov

224

The Hermitage was target No. 9 on the maps of the gunmen shelling the besieged city.

Portico of the entrance to the New Hermitage
Photograph of 1944

As the elderly Nikolai Tikhonov, doyen of Soviet poets, wrote in May 1942: "Anyone who had seen Leningrad in January or February would fail to recognize the city today. Then streets were buried in snow drifts, long icicles drooped from the eaves, pavements were completely frozen over, piles of filth lay everywhere, garbage cluttered up the courtyards, and roads were strewn with rubble. Now, one may walk along the broad streets and splendid embankments, swept clean as if by one gigantic broom. This was no simple job, no easy chore. Day after day three hundred thousand Leningraders worked from dawn till dusk to clear away the snow, ice, muck and rubble. This was another gallant exploit of labour, one the world had never seen before, that was accomplished by the people of Leningrad. The Augean Stables were child's play compared with this stupendous feat done by the people worn down by a terrible winter."

Hermitage staff also pitched in that spring, despite the rigours of the blockade, despite the hunger and the weariness. They had handled pick, shovel and broom before, when keeping the roadway of the Palace Embankment free for army traffic, as along with other thoroughfares, it was right behind the frontline. Now their job was to clear the entire sprawling

225

The atlantes at the entrance
to the New Hermitage

226

The New Hermitage
War-time photograph

227

The New Hermitage

226

227

228, 229

In March 1942 all the windows of the Main Staircase of the Winter Palace were shattered by a bomb blast. Shattered glass lay on the marble steps, snow was falling on the statues of muses and deities.

The Main Staircase in the Winter Palace

230

The ceiling painting of the Main Staircase in the Winter Palace before the restoration

231

The painted ceiling, depicting the sun-lit Olympus, became almost black.

The Main Staircase in the Winter Palace. Ceiling painting: *Olympus*

230

229

grounds of the Hermitage buildings of the ice and the snow, the muck and the rubbish, scouring every single cluttered-up yard, attic and cellar, every sewage pipe, every nook or cranny where there might be filth, as in the rays of the spring sun anything of this order could develop into a breeding ground of contagion and disease...

There was now a new heading in the daybook for the *Transactions of the Hermitage*, which read: "Progress of work to clear Hermitage grounds." Most of this work was done by the womenfolk, as towards spring hardly any men were left on the Hermitage staff; they could be counted on the fingers of one's hands, and their number included some who were well over sixty. The youngest among them was Pavel Gubchevsky, who had been given a complete discharge from army service because of a serious cardiac defect.

After the war broke out, this man, who was a researcher, a guide and a lecturer, had his hands full, both literally and figuratively. He helped to pack and crate paintings and other works of art, organized the transportation of the evacuated Hermitage treasures to the

railway station, served as a fire-watching warden on the rooftop, and assisted in bringing down the unevacuated items to the ground floor and cellars for safekeeping. In the spring of 1942, in March, when Professor Dobroklonsky was appointed the new Head Keeper of the Hermitage, he was appointed chief of the museum guard. The following 1942 archival document provides some indication of the conditions in which he was obliged to carry out his duties:

"On the guard payroll are sixty-four people of whom only forty-six report for duty (before the war there were 650 persons on the guard payroll). Guards are posted outside and inside the building in daytime and night shifts. They watch over around one million cubic metres of space, a display territory fifteen kilometres long, and 1,057 rooms in the Winter Palace alone. Currently, the guarding of inner premises is more complicated as due to the destruction caused by the shelling, a number of premises may be easily infiltrated."

Gubchevsky describes the situation in greater detail: "My mighty troop was composed mostly of elderly ladies of fifty-five years of age and more, including some who were seventy. Many were cripples who before the war

232

Gallery of the History of Antique Painting
Photograph of 1944

233

Gallery of the History of Antique Painting during the siege of Leningrad
Drawing by Vasily Kuchumov. 1942

234

235

had served as museum room attendants, as a limp or some other disfigurement did not interfere then with their job of seeing to it that proper order was maintained. However, by the spring of 1942, many had left and as many had died. The living continued to discharge guard duty. On the payroll were some fifty guards, but, as a rule, at least a third would be in hospital. Hence, the guard squad that I commanded never exceeded, in effect, some thirty feeble-bodied elderly ladies. Such was my valiant troop."

These thirty elderly ladies stood guard over the buildings of the Hermitage, at the gates and doorways and in the rooms, round the clock. The rest of the museum staff was likewise few in number, but a fifth of what it had been before the war. In April 1942, those who could still walk and whose age allowed them to be conscripted for municipal jobs, cleared away the embankment, yards and attics. It had been planned

237

238

239, 241

Beneath the stones of the nameless graves of the Piskariovskoye Memorial Cemetery,
where the Eternal Flame burns in commemoration of the dead Leningraders, lie the remains
of many who had once been on the Hermitage staff. Some were young, budding scholars,
others were researchers of world repute, some were the elderly ladies from among
the room attendants, others were joiners and electricians. Incised in the granite are the words:
"Nobody is forgotten, nothing is forgotten."

Piskariovskoye Memorial Cemetery

П р и к а з

по Государственному Эрмитажу

№ 26

Ленинград   "4" марта 1942 г.

§ 1.

Исключаются из списков сотрудников Эрмитажа, за смертью:

1. Вахтер т. Титов Д.А. с 8.II с.г.

2. Ст. реставратор т. Альбрехт Л.П. с 22.II с.г.

3. Ст.научн.сотр. т. Соколова Е.П. с 28.II с.г.

4. Аспирант т. Птицын Г.В. с 2.II с.г.

5. Монтер по отоплению т. Ростовцов И.А. с 18.II с.г.

6. Муз.-техн.рабочий т. Ткач Ф.Д. с 2.III с.г.

7. Постовой охраны т. Богданов Л.Г. с 19.II с.г.

8. Постовая охраны т. Богданова П.Т. с 19.II с.г.

9. Плотник т. Каретников И.Я. с 18.II с.г.

10. Муз.-техн.раб. т. Большакова О.А. с 16.II с.г.

11. Муз.-техн. раб. т. Васильев И.В. с 3.II с.г.

12. Монтер т. Соболев Ф.В. с 5.II с.г.

13. Плотник т. Дозоров Ф.В. с 30.1 с.г.

14. Постовая охраны т. Летина А.Ф. с 19.II с.г.

15. Постовая охраны т. Волхонская О.А. с 21.II с.г.

16. Бухгалтер т. Буц Р.Я. с 21.II с.г.

17. Постовая охраны т. Карягина М.М. с 24.II с.г.

18. Постовая охраны т. Дзякович Е.А. с 27.II с.г.

19. Водопроводчик т. Смирнов П.Д. с 20.II с.г.

240

241

239

240

Extract from a 1942 Hermitage notice citing
the names of the dead Hermitage workers

to do the indoor cleaning after the grounds had been tidied, but the arrival of spring in full force necessitated immediate emergency work inside the Hermitage buildings.

With the arrival of spring, the fanciful patterns of hoarfrost traced on the walls and ceilings inside the Hermitage no longer coruscated like diamonds when a ray of sunshine, refracted in a still intact window pane, impinged upon the still ice-cold marble. The spring thaw breathed a damp warmth into the frozen air inside, with the result that the silvery crystal myriads darkened to transform into millions of beads of dull moisture which dripped down the walls in rivulets of filth and dirt.

Meanwhile the snow on the rooftops melted away to release more rivulets of water that dripped through the fragment-riddled roofs. From the attics the water ran down further into the rooms themselves, splotching the ceilings and their painted panels with dark and ugly stains. The pails and basins that were strategically placed in the attics did not help much, as they filled to overflowing almost the moment they were emptied. Everything humanly possible was done to patch over the rents in the roofs with burlap and sacking, but the moment one hole was plugged up, another would appear somewhere else.

The condition of the rooms having large skylights was simply catastrophic. They had no attic or corrugated roofing and the flying shell and bomb splinters and the blasts from explosions had shattered practically every pane of glass. So, when the snow that had piled up during the winter

242

In spring the museum workers with crowbars, shovels and brooms came out into the streets to clean the territory around the Hermitage of snow, ice and dirt.

Cleaning the territory in front of the New Hermitage
Drawing by Nikolai Pavlov. 1942

243

The granite atlantes bore on their mighty shoulders the massive cornice of the Hermitage portal, a cornice scarred by a deep fissure; the people protecting the Hermitage were no atlantes, on the contrary, they were gaunt and feeble for want of food and warmth. But on their frail shoulders they bore the whole of the Hermitage.

Cleaning one of the rooms in the spring of 1942
Drawing by Vera Miliutina

ВМ.
1942
Уборка Залов Эрмитажа

245

244

Desk and arm-chair of poplarwood
Russia. 19th century

245

Furniture of rosewood inlaid with porcelain
Russia. The Gambs factory. 1846

246

*The Hermitage halls and storerooms contain
a rich collection of furniture. Part of it was not
evacuated — in spring its upholstery was covered
with mould.*

Drying the furniture
Photograph of 1942

247

April, 1942
Drawing by Vera Miliutina

248

The Hall of Twelve Columns in the New Hermitage had long been called the Coin Hall. It was on its high open gallery that the treasures of the Numismatic Department were packed during the first days of the war.

The Hall of Twelve Columns in the New Hermitage Built by Vasily Stasov and Nikolai Yefimov after Leo von Klenze's design. 1842–51

249

A hole caused by a direct hit in the ceiling of the Hall of Twelve Columns where in June 1941 the coins and medals were being packed.

Photograph of 1944

250

Russian coins. In the centre, silver bars that were in circulation before coins were minted

251

Western European medals. 15th–19th centuries

252

Yulia Arkhipova. Born 1930
Medal from the series *Leningrad during the Siege*. 1974

253

Drawers for keeping coins in the Department of Numismatics

252

253

on top of the skylight frames began to melt in the spring sunshine, the drip swelled into a deluge that splashed down upon the parquet flooring of the central rooms of the Picture Gallery. There it combined with the sand strewn all around to create one vast sea of mud.

The elderly lady curators climbed up onto the roofs and tried to lash plywood boards to the skylight frames with wire. However, each sharp gust of wind would dislodge the boards and then again the melting snow was dripping down to warp, buckle and swell the parquet floors inside.

The damp had mounted a spring offensive. The painted ceiling panels darkened and moisture accumulated on the walls, mirrors and columns. Having squeezed into pails the soaking rags with which they tried to suck up the moisture, the little old ladies went outside to help clear the yards.

Many of the cellars, where valuable works of art had been stored, also necessitated rush emergency work, triggered off, firstly, by the breakdown in the basement beneath the Athena Room, where, as you will no doubt remember, the unevacuated porcelain had been stowed away.

The Coin Room
Watercolour by Ludwig Premazzi. 1853

During two hundred years or so these exquisite figurines of coquettish marquises and shepherdesses and of elegant cavaliers and modish dandies, whose biscuit bodies had been tempered in the heat of the muffle kilns of Meissen and Sèvres, had gone through more than one ordeal of storm and stress. However, in the depths of their gloomy cellar, steeped waist high in a bed of sand alongside vases, chandeliers and services for every occasion, they quietly survived Leningrad's first siege winter, only shuddering in one tempo when from time to time their refuge quaked down to its very foundations, and then once again settled into immobility. However, with the coming of spring misfortune struck. The water pipes burst in their seemingly so dependable hideaway, and streams of water gushed in.

"I was literally terrified when I saw that all the porcelain had been flooded," Olga Mikhailova, art historian and critic, recalled. "In rubber waders we descended into the dark cellar. The water reached up to our knees. Placing each foot down carefully, so as not to tread on these fragile objects, we felt around to pluck out object after object. Some of the dishes and plates floated on the surface. Though the necks of some of the taller vases jutted out above the water, most of the items, which were clogged up with

255

Bomb blast smashed the frames piled on the gallery of the Coach-house, shell splinters thrusting into the stone vaults.

The Coach-house in the Small Hermitage
Photograph of 1944

256

"Vis-à-vis" coach
France. 18th century

A 70-mm shell exploded in the Coach-house.
Photograph of 1944

sand and filth, had settled on the floor. Much later, recalling these searches in the darkness, our wading in the water, and also how we, loaded with these porcelain objects, had climbed the dark steep steps, feeling the way with feet only, we could hardly believe it. It seemed as if we had pulled off incredible acrobatic stunts, and we were really and truly amazed that not once did we break anything.

"Having rescued the porcelain, we tried to rid it of all the accumulated muck. Though they were not the gems of the Hermitage collection, still every piece was a true work of art. We found it easy enough to wipe the glazed items clean. But as for the biscuit pieces, their unglazed white china had absorbed the water and had yellowed. Further, many items that earlier had gone through the restorer's hands had come apart. Finally many of the objects had come out of the water without their respective inventory labels, of which hundreds floated around, and that could have caused terrible confusion. We were forced to do everything at once; to wash, wipe clean and restore the inventory label. We left the porcelain to dry out in the yard in the spring sunshine on top of sacking or right out on the greening grass."

Spring also caused deterioration of the prized articles of antique furniture, which had been transferred the previous autumn into the former palace mews. The frosted walls exuded a dampness that filled the air and was soaked up by the wood. As a result the furniture oozed moisture and the upholstery was covered with mildew. "We made use of every sunny day," Alexandra Anosova recalled, "to drag out all the upholstered furniture into the courtyard. The upholstery on the couches and chairs was covered with a thick, furry layer of mildew, as if these pieces of furniture had been upholstered not in velvet and silk but in some revolting, hideous yellow-green sheepskin. The sundried mildew was brushed off and all day long clouds of dust and the acrid fumes of sulphide filled the air so much so that towards evening our clothes reeked of it, while the dust choked eyes, ears and nose and rasped the throat."

The sun now rode high in the skies, radiating an increasing warmth. In between the towering palace buildings — scarred by broken cornices, peeling stucco and heavily pocked masonry — there were ranged in the inner courtyards, right out in the open, antique pieces of furniture crafted of such precious woods as mahogany, rosewood and Karelian birch; in fact, chairs made in the reigns of Catherine the Great, the Emperor Paul I and the Emperor

258

259

258

The Pavilion Hall.
Detail of architectural decor

259

A pile of sand and a shovel became a permanent detail of the Hermitage interior during the siege.

Photograph of 1941

260

In January 1943 the mosaics of the Pavilion Hall were covered with bumpy ice.

Copy of the mosaic floor found during the excavations of the thermae in Ocriculum near Rome in 1780

261

Alexander I ringed the slopes of that mountain of sand which had piled up in the Hermitage courtyard opening on to the Winter Canal, and on top of it, enjoying the warmth, the elderly ladies from the museum guard perched. As they sat there, stretching out scurvy-swollen black-splotched legs, they listened to the explosions of bursting shells, now faraway, now quite close at hand.

The enemy resumed aerial bombing of the city in the spring. Shelling was also intensive and heavy; between April and June there were but eighteen days when there was no gunfire.

Pavel Gubchevsky recalled: "After each enemy bombing attack and round of shelling, my colleagues and I necessarily undertook a tour of inspection.

262

263

264

This was essential, as during the thunder and roar one could easily over-look even something serious, so extensive was the area in our charge. One day, when inspecting the building of the New Hermitage, I entered the Hall of Twelve Columns, which had housed our Department of Numismatics before the war. As I looked around, I spotted a jagged hole from a direct hit above the gallery where we had packed the coins and medals. As far as I could judge, this had not occurred on that day. Now my route was much longer than that of the excursions I had guided before the war. As I made my way through the maze of galleries, stairs and passages, I felt dizzy, the result of the hungry winter I had endured, and I couldn't help

The last of the thirty shells that hit the Hermitage buildings exploded in the Armorial Hall.

Photograph of 1944

266, 267

Painters, plasterers, gilders and moulders will soon return the Armorial Hall to its pristine beauty.

The Armorial Hall in the Winter Palace Designed by Vasily Stasov. 1837–39

265

266

thinking to myself that if I were to fall, my dead body would be found perhaps a year, or at best, half a year, later, somewhere here, in this remote nook, far from the usual Hermitage pathways."

In May two bulky parcels arrived from Moscow from the Committee for Art Affairs. They contained vitamins — twenty pots of vitamin C dissolved in a syrup of invert sugar, plus five hundred tubes of the same vitamin with a glucose additive. The vitamins were distributed among the most emaciated, scurvy-stricken and all whose bodies had been

mottled with black splotches from a vitamin deficiency. In that same month the Hermitage staff planted in the grounds a kitchen garden to grow such vitamin-rich vegetables as carrots, cabbage and onions. As a matter of fact that spring all of Leningrad, all its gardens, parks and boulevards, were turned into vegetable gardens, with rows of vegetables planted on the Field of Mars, in the Summer Gardens, on the lawns around the statues and monuments, and on the vacant plots in between the bomb- and shell-razed houses. The Hermitage staff planted their vegetable garden in the Hanging Garden on the first floor.

Even in the age of sumptuous luxury of the eighteenth century, this Hanging Garden, arranged above the palace mews by a whim of Catherine the Great, had evoked the admiration of the foreign envoys and Russian aristocrats invited to the Winter Palace. One enters it through a

267   268

268
The Armorial Hall
Photograph of 1944

glass door leading from the Pavilion Hall of the Small Hermitage and from that point it runs parallel to the Gallery of Peter the Great and the Romanov Gallery; indeed, the Garden itself resembles an unroofed museum gallery, with marble statuary gleaming white amidst the trees, shrubs and flower-beds. The last time the lilacs blossomed there had been in the summer of 1941; the rose bushes and trees died later in autumn. True, when spring arrived again, the lilac bushes again turned green, but no longer to burst into blossom. "We," Olga Mikhailova recalled, "ripped out the bushes of lilac and honeysuckle to make way for our vegetable garden. As, day after day, we dug the earth and planted the vegetables, the

269

Icon of Our Lady of Kazan. Russia. Late 18th century

270
Gold chalice. Russia. 1901

271
Silver gilt service. Russia. 1840s

torn-out bushes lay by the wall, with clods of earth still clinging to their roots, and slowly withered. During that blockade spring we witnessed many a death. The lilacs of the Hermitage also died a long and torturous death." The rows of vegetables in the Hanging Garden were assiduously watered and weeded, and the earth was rid of the shell splinters that rained down upon it each time Nazi gunners trained their artillery on the Winter Palace.

Nazi long-range artillery bombarded the Winter Palace. Thus, on May 8 an enemy shell exploded in the place where the mildewed furniture was being cleaned; by pure chance, none of the museum staff were there at the moment, but a member of the fire-fighting team was killed on the spot.

A week later, on May 14, shells hit the ground-floor wall on the side facing the Admiralty, and the roof over the Saltykov Staircase and exploded outside the Main Entrance, which opens onto the Palace Embankment, and also amidst the trees in the Great Courtyard of the Winter Palace. One more shell slammed into the wall of the depository of antique coaches on the ground floor of the de La Mothe Pavilion, which is beneath the Romanov Gallery and the Hanging Garden; though it did not breach the wall, it nevertheless heavily mauled

272

273

272

The Armorial Hall
Drawing by Vasily Kuchumov. 1942

273

The Armorial Hall. A hole in the floor
Photograph of 1944

274

The Rastrelli Gallery. A hole
in the ceiling
Photograph of 1944

the masonry. Veteran soldiers claim that a second shell or bomb will never hit the crater produced by an earlier shell or bomb. However, the war-time chronicles of the Hermitage Museum refute that claim. Indeed, on June 18, a mere month later, a 70 mm-calibre shell struck the very same spot where the brickwork of the Coach-house wall had been wrecked, now to explode inside, blasting into smithereens seven carriages and two palanquin litters and wreaking extensive damage amongst all the other items of this unique collection that had been once housed in the Carriages Museum. It had boasted some magnificent specimens of the coachmaker's art of the eighteenth century, both Russian and foreign: the state coaches of the Empress Catherine the Great and the Emperor Paul I, gala carriages, travelling equipages, phaetons, traps, palace landaus, litters, sledges and sleighs, ornamented with bronze, gilded and carved scroll-work and lacquer painting.

275

A heavy bronze chandelier from the Peter the Great Hall was smashed beyond repair by a bomb blast; it was replaced by a silver one.

Photograph of 1944

276, 277

At the beginning of the war Lyon velvet was removed from the walls, rolled over rollers and evacuated.

The Peter the Great Hall, or the Small Throne Room, in the Winter Palace Designed by Auguste Montferrand, 1833; rebuilt by Vasily Stasov, 1837–38

275

That spring the *Pole Star* yacht, which throughout the winter had supplied the Hermitage with some amount of electricity, weighed anchor and sailed away. Professor Dobroklonsky at once despatched an urgent message to Smolny that read: "The complete lack of electric lighting deprives the Hermitage staff of possibilities of doing any work at all! Should it be impossible to provide electric lighting, then please instruct that supplies of kerosene be issued to the Hermitage."

But as the Hermitage had been "mothballed," it continued to be cut off from the mains; the electricity generated by the municipal power plants barely sufficed to keep the factories going, light the hospitals, and power the trams that were now going once again. It was dark and gloomy inside the Hermitage, especially because of the boarded-up windows, which let in neither the bright June sunlight nor the pale glow of the white nights. However, supplies of kerosene oil were delivered and until autumn, when the icebreaker *Yermak* dropped anchor off the Palace Embankment and an

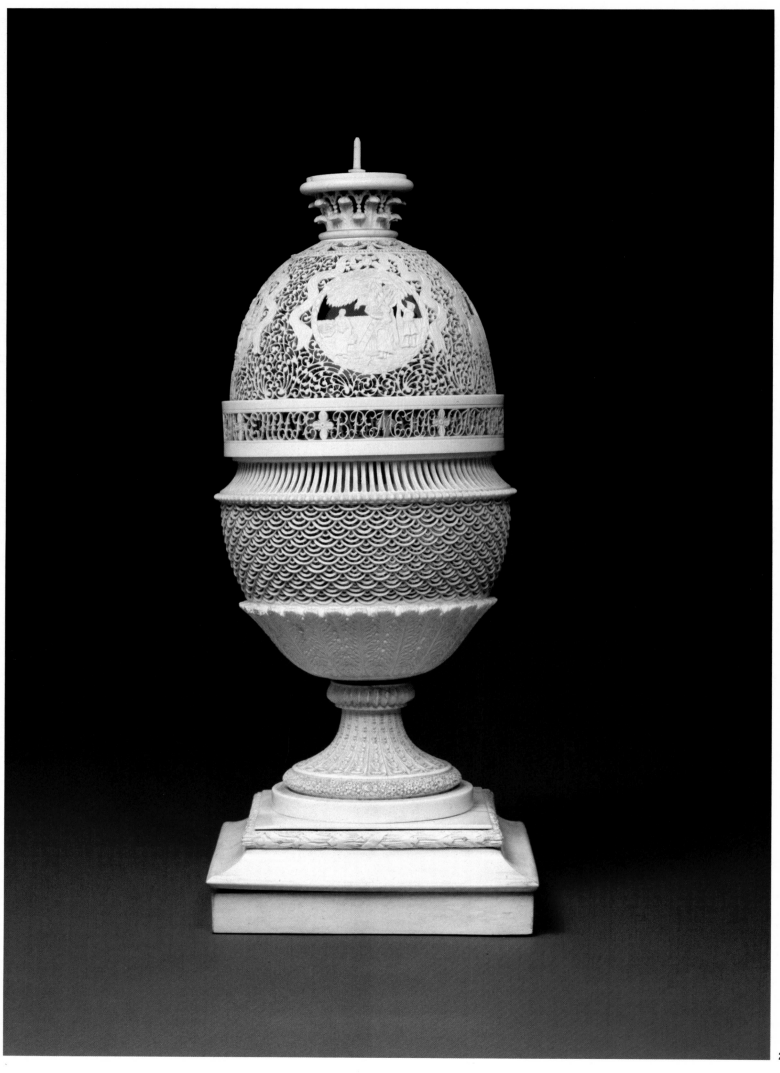

279   280

281

278

Vase with the seasons of the year.
Russia. By Nikolai Vereshchagin.
Late 18th century

279, 280

Grigory Musikiysky.
1670/71 – after 1739
Russia. Enamel miniatures on gold

281

Russian enamels
Solvychegodsk. Late 18th century

electric cable was once again laid across to connect the Hermitage Museum with its power generators, kerosene lanterns burned round the clock. In the light of these lamps, "the curators, professors and researchers," an official document states, "perform every conceivable job required to 'mothball' the establishment, transferring valuable collections to drier premises and examining items with a view to protecting rugs and carpets, tapestries, textiles, etc., from moths, and metal from corrosion and tin plague."

Towards evening, extinguishing their lanterns, the curators, professors and researchers would come to the Hanging Garden to water and weed their vegetable patches. That done, they returned to their respective desks, relit the lanterns and pulled out of the drawers the books and manuscripts needed. Sundown, blocked from view behind the boarded-up windows, hastened, as is always the case during Leningrad's white nights, to meet sunrise, likewise obscured by the sheets of plywood that had replaced the blown-out window-panes. The new day began with the six-o'clock news

282, 283

The 1812 Gallery in the Winter Palace
Designed by Carlo Rossi, 1826; rebuilt
by Vasily Stasov, 1839

284

The 1812 Gallery during the siege of Leningrad
Drawing by Vasily Kuchumov. 1942

285

The Knights' Hall in the New Hermitage. Medieval knights stand on the pedestals, their armour displayed at the showcases.

The Knights' Hall in the New Hermitage
Built by Vasily Stasov and Nikolai Yefimov after
Leo von Klenze's design. 1842–51

286

The Knights' Hall. Western European arms and armour

287

Rapier
Italy. Early 17th century

288

When the war broke out the Hermitage knights were displayed in St George Hall. The picture shows them without their armour, with piles of sand in between the pedestals.
Tatyana Tess: "Right in front at the door stood as sentinels two medieval knights who had been stripped of all their armour... By their side were crates of sand, axes, crowbars and a pair of enormous pincers."

St George Hall during the siege
Watercolour by Vera Miliutina

and the Soviet Information Bureau's morning communiqué, and again the staff went down into the cellars and the storage rooms, into the halls to board up shattered windows again, or up to the roof to patch over the rents and holes. The Hermitage knew no respite in its war effort, no letdown in the day-to-day fight against the treacherous dampness lethal for the museum's exhibits and buildings. Having repelled the furious spring onslaught of melting snow, the Hermitage staff now girded themselves to resist the fierce offensive of the autumn downpours and the ferocious attack of the winter blizzards.

The granite atlantes bore on their mighty shoulders the massive cornice of the Hermitage portal, a cornice scarred by a deep fissure, a gaping wound in the stone. The people protecting the Hermitage were no atlantes; on the contrary, they were gaunt and feeble for want of food and warmth. But on their frail shoulders they bore not just one cornice but the whole of the Hermitage Museum.

This time winter was not winter as Russians know it. Snow had fallen onto Leningrad's rooftops back in November, but in December it melted. There was nothing but muck, slush and a foggy gloom. When would Lake Ladoga become ice-bound? When would the Road of Life across its ice get going again this winter?

The enemy still stood on the approaches to the city, at its very walls, as a year earlier, in the winter of 1941. Heavy siege artillery continued to lob shells into Leningrad. The howitzers and mortars of the enemy were trained also on the Hermitage and the Winter Palace. Thus, on November 28 three shells exploded in the courtyards, the blast causing the museum buildings to quake and shudder. However, in that same month there came to the ears of the Hermitage Museum staff the distant peal of another battle fought far from the city, the victorious battle on the Volga. The grand victories that Soviet forces won on the banks of that mother of Russia's rivers signified a turn of the tide in the war. Joyful, gladdening changes could now be anticipated on the banks of the Neva, too.

December passed and the new year of 1943 dawned. On the night of January 18, the jubilant voice of the announcer kindled joy in the hearts of Leningraders: "The blockade of Leningrad has been broken," he declared in sonorous, ringing tones.

The encirclement of the city was broken south of Lake Ladoga, and on this narrow strip of liberated land a railway was laid down, which again linked Leningrad with the mainland. Meanwhile on the other sectors, the enemy was still standing at the city's very gates. It would take a long, weary year before the city would be completely rid of the ring of the Nazi blockade. There would yet be a whole year of trial and tribulation for Leningrad's people, including the staff of the Hermitage Museum.

"Because of the heavy damage recently sustained by the Hermitage, much more work had to be done. During the first three months of 1943 the Hermitage staff manually removed from the buildings some eighty tons of broken glass and snow." Eighty tons. What did that really mean? The pertinent document has no mention whatever that the eighty tons "manually removed" included tons of ice chipped off not from pavements in the vicinity nor even from the courtyards but from the walls and floors and ceilings of the rooms.

"The following happened about a week after the blockade was broken," Pavel Gubchevsky recalled. "Late in the evening of January 25, a Nazi Junkers dropped a one-ton high-explosive bomb on Palace Square. The blast caused the massive building of the Winter Palace to rock like a cockleshell on a storm-ridden, choppy sea. All the Hermitage buildings were subjected to the monstrous force of the explosion. Whirling across the Hanging Garden, the shock wave burst into the Pavilion Hall and blew out all window panes, even those facing the Neva. The blizzard that raged later that night whirled through the empty frames of the broken windows, sweeping in twirling eddies of damp snow that settled down on the floors, covering it with a blanket of white fluff. Next morning it thawed, but at night a severe frost struck and the snow froze with the bits of broken glass, strewn on the floor, to create one solid crust of ice. Our first thought was to save the parquetry and mosaics on the floors

289 The enemy being defeated near Leningrad, the tanks are moved to other sectors of the front

290 The siege is lifted! Salute on January 27, 1944

292 Leningraders are listening to the announcement of the end of the war

from devastation. My job was to take care of the Pavilion Hall, where a thick layer of knobby ice and chips of shattered glass obscured the magnificent mosaic adorning the floor in front of the doors leading out into the Hanging Garden. Working with a small iron crowbar I gingerly chipped the ice and glass away, inch by inch."

One could hear crowbars picking away at the ice in the other rooms too. Tons of ice and glass were trundled out of the museum on handbarrows.

The Hermitage staff had no respite, even though between January and mid-May there were no direct bombing attacks or shelling of the museum. Still, though no bombs rained down, there were the spring showers that came extremely early, in February, carried in by the masses of warm air that blew in from an unexpected quarter. They were a real calamity for the Hermitage, which had gone unheated through two winters.

The warm moisture of early spring, which oozed from the frozen walls, saturated the inside air and settled, more intensively than during the spring of 1942, on the cold marble, the mirrors, the bronze mountings and the stone vases. The moulding cracked off the ceilings and the cornices, and the gilding of the Main Staircase lost its glitter and peeled; the paint hung suspended in ragged tufts from the denuded, rusting metal beneath.

The entire spring was one long exhausting fight against the dampness. Everything humanly possible was undertaken to repel and resist the attacking moisture, to protect the treasures of the Hermitage from corrosion and the tin plague, from the mildew and the furniture beetle, from swelling and peeling paint, in short from every conceivable ravage that the second war-time spring again menaced the museum with.

Least trouble of all during that nerve-racking season was caused by the three-thousand-year-old mummy of the Egyptian priest Petese which remained in the Hermitage — only from time to time some amount of salts would be exuded, which would at once be tidily wiped off, the keepers never ceasing to appreciate the high degree of skill that embalmers had displayed in the days of the pharaohs. Nor was any particular effort needed to take care of the carcasses of the horses that archaeologists had extracted from the burial mounds in the Altai, where two thousand five hundred years of interment in permafrost had forever preserved them from the ravages of time. But whereas the dampness of Leningrad's spring held no peril for the desiccated mummy of the Egyptian priest or for the hides of the war-chargers of Pazyryk, the scores of thousands of articles so superbly wrought in metal and clay, or carved from wood, or woven of strands of wool and silk, or painted in oils and watercolours, or drawn in charcoal and pastel, engravings, in short, these scores of thousands of exquisite works of art insistently demanded a new refuge without dripping walls and flooded floors.

Hence, all that could be carried on one's back, all that could be dragged along, all that many hands could at once lift or lower, was trundled into drier premises. Except for the antique pieces of furniture which continued to fill the former palace mews beneath the Hanging Garden. None of the Hermitage staff had the physical energy left to move out these massive wardrobes and chests. And so they hoped against hope that perchance the piercing, marrow-chilling draughts and frequent and long airing would oust the dampness.

While draughts blew in and out of the furniture depository, up above, in the Hanging Garden, the spring sunshine melted the snow. There was nothing new about that. Spring had melted snow in this spot for more than a hundred years now, but the coat of lead laid beneath the metre-thick layer of soil had afforded an impenetrable barrier to the thawing snow. At one time a number of slender saplings had been planted there, but with the passage of time they had grown into mighty spreading trees—which, however, had to be removed the moment the gardeners noticed that their powerful roots had reached the lead plating beneath and were using their irrepressible vital juices to bore further into it. The damaged waterproofing had been scheduled for a general overhaul in 1941; however, the war intervened. Thus far all had passed off rather smoothly while the drainage system was still functioning normally; however, it so happened that in the spring of 1943 the upright pipes which

294

293

Cleaning the embankment near
the Winter Palace
Photograph of 1944

294

Glassing the windows in the Gallery
of the History of Antique Painting
Photograph of 1944

295

The Gallery of the History of Antique Painting
in the Hermitage
Built by Vasily Stasov and Nikolai Yefimov
after Leo von Klenze's design. 1842–51

had drained the water off from the Hanging Garden into the special conduits had clogged up with refuse and ice; as a result, the sun-thawed snow streamed through the holes that the roots of the trees had bored into the lead sheathing; from there it penetrated into the storey below, and, thence, into the palace mews in one unending deluge.

When that occurred a company of army school cadets was specially despatched to the rescue. These young men had but recently been moved into Leningrad across Lake Ladoga, to go through a course of officer training at one of the army schools in this frontline city and subsequently command platoons and sections in the forthcoming fighting to achieve the full liberation of Leningrad from the Nazi grip. This was their first visit to the Hermitage; however, they trooped in not through the Main Entrance as had been the case in pre-war times but through the side gates. Here they were shown furniture of great beauty, although soaking wet, and they at once started carrying it from the former palace mews to the former palace hall, where the mummified remains of horses lay behind the glass windows of museum showcases. Here, a man in civvies, who introduced himself as the chief of the museum guards, briefly explained that some two and a half thousand years ago the chieftains of warlike nomad tribes had galloped on these steeds across the vast Altai steppes; the furniture that they were now carrying into the premises of the Department of Prehistoric Culture had been crafted during the reigns of the French kings Louis XIV, Louis XV, and Louis XVI.

ГОСУДАРСТВЕННЫЙ ЭРМИТАЖ
приглашает Вас на открытие
ВРЕМЕННОЙ ВЫСТАВКИ

ПАМЯТНИКОВ ИСКУССТВА И КУЛЬТУРЫ,

ХРАНИВШИХСЯ В ЛЕНИНГРАДЕ

ВО ВРЕМЯ БЛОКАДЫ   на 2 лица

ОТКРЫТИЕ ВЫСТАВКИ

состоится

8-го Ноября 1944 г. в 13 час.

Вход с Советского подъезда.
Дворцовая набережная, д. 34

297

298

298

Academician Orbeli assumed personal direction
of all preparatory work for the exhibition.

Photograph of 1944

Their job done, the cadets departed, leaving the chief of the Hermitage guards behind with his "mighty troop" of little old ladies, who continued to maintain their vigil, while other members of the staff continued to carry, scrub and dry the Hermitage pieces. On May 12, those members of the Hermitage staff occupied with the planting of vegetables in the Hanging Garden suddenly heard the unfortunately all-too-familiar roar of an enemy plane somewhere high up beyond the clouds. It dived, circled several times above the Neva, buzzed the Winter Palace almost at roof-height and, its engines roaring, receded again into the clouds. At this moment one of the ARP wardens reported that smoke was billowing forth in the Kitchen Yard, where apparently something was on fire.

301

301

301

It was necessary to clean the rooms and galleries intended for the temporary exhibition of sand and rubbish.

The Pavilion Hall during the siege
Drawing by Vasily Kuchumov

302

All the twenty-eight cut-glass chandeliers were repaired and put in their original places, the floors were polished as before the war.

The Pavilion Hall in the Small Hermitage
Designed by Andrei Stakenschneider. 1850—58

299, 300

A strip of red carpet is to be put on the white marble steps of the Councillors' Staircase, which will take the visitors of the first exhibition after the war to the Pavilion Hall.

The Councillors' Staircase in the Old Hermitage
Designed by Andrei Stakenschneider. 1850—58

"What we feared most of all was fire," Pavel Gubchevsky recalled. "Whereas a bomb or shell might destroy part of a building, fire had the tendency to spread. I was well familiar with the history of the Winter Palace, and despite all the worries of the war-time siege never forgot the fearful fire that more than a hundred years earlier, in 1837, had ravaged the Winter Palace, destroying everything that could be destroyed. By the time I reached the Kitchen Yard the clouds of smoke had dispersed. A few minutes later the municipal fire chiefs arrived. We intently examined the spot, but did not see anything burning. Nor could we catch the smell of fire. The firemen left, but I still felt worried. Once again we looked intently around and I suddenly noticed a broken window on the ground floor where our storerooms are located. It at once came to mind that at night a burglar had climbed in with felonious intent. Dragging a step-ladder to the spot, I climbed the steps and peered inside. You can well imagine how startled I was to see

a quarter-ton bomb lying amidst the scattered paintings on a bed of torn canvases and shattered stretchers. Only later did I come to realize what had actually happened. It appeared that the bomb the Nazi bomber had dropped had hit the eaves of the building across the yard, however not with its detonator but with its casing. Under the impact the hundred-year-old masonry had crumbled into dust and had raised a thick cloud. Meanwhile the bomb itself had ricochetted and fell into the window, but again sideways, and then had come to rest, without exploding, on a disarrayed stack of paintings."

The Hermitage ARP wardens at once cordoned off the Kitchen Yard and all approaches thereto; army sappers were immediately summoned. The quarter-ton bomb was defused and carted away. Now the curators took over and recorded the following: "As a result of a direct hit by a high-explosive bomb in the picture depository of the Department of Russian Culture, some paintings were completely destroyed and more were severely damaged. The pictures have been transferred into adjacent storage rooms, and restoration of the most valuable pieces as well as the registration of the losses incurred has begun."

303

View of the Winter Palace from the Admiralty

In autumn, when the last potato had been dug out of the vegetable plot in the Hanging Garden, the barrage balloons were still high up in the skies and the gunfire had still not abated. However, Radio Moscow already broadcast jubilant communiqués reporting Soviet advances in many sectors. As the third war-time winter approached, Leningraders, indeed the entire country, had the mounting conviction that soon the enemy would be put to rout at the walls of the city. Very soon now...

While the enemy was still bombarding the besieged city, its Party and Government leadership decided to open a school to train highly-skilled specialists such as builders, house-painters, painters, moulders, stained-glass artists, marble cutters, mosaicists, woodcarvers, gilders, goldsmiths, and cabinet-makers. They would do restoration work and other highly delicate decoration on the buildings both residential and public that were damaged during the siege. It was understood that all these specialists would soon carry out restoration and other work on the Hermitage Museum, too...

That was, indeed, imminent. Soon too, the supplies of plywood petered out. But now the Hermitage Museum chief engineer was not so worried

304

Roof-makers have started repairing the roofs pierced by shell splinters.

Photograph of 1944

305

306

305, 307

The Early Italian Renaissance Room
in the Old Hermitage
Designed by Andrei Stakenschneider. 1851–54

306

*Thousands of exquisite works of art insistently demanded
a new refuge without dripping walls and flooded floors.
Hence, all that could be carried on one's back, all that
could be dragged along, all that many hands could
at once lift or lower, was trundled into drier premises.*

Drying the pictures in the rooms of Italian art
in the Old Hermitage
War-time photograph

308

Iosif Orbeli with a group
of Hermitage workers
Photograph of 1945

309

Lorries at the Main Entrance
to the Hermitage
Photograph of 1945

310

Soviet Army soldiers are helping
to unload boxes with the Hermitage
exhibits
Photograph of 1945

311

Examining the re-evacuated exhibits
Photograph of 1945

312

Vase. Kettle. Cup and a saucer
Russia. 1825–50

313

Porcelain statuettes
Meissen, Germany.
18th century

314

Chinese enamels. 17th–18th
centuries

315

Figure of a lion with a cub
China. Ch'ing dynasty, reign
of K'ang-hsi (1662–1722)

314

315

on discovering that no plywood was left, as he had good reason to think that some of the window panes, installed long before the war, were seemingly under the magic spell of a kind wizard and would last until the war was over. He was overly optimistic. "An enemy shell that exploded in the courtyard of the Winter Palace on December 16 blew out up to 750 square metres of glass, including windows in the Armorial Hall, the Hall of Field Marshals, the Peter the Great Hall and other premises with opulently decorated interiors," Professor Mikhail Dobroklonsky stated in his report to Leningrad's mayor. "The State Hermitage Museum requests assistance in the procurement of 5.5 cubic metres of plywood."

316

Antique glass
Levant, Italy. 1st–4th centuries

317

Preparing objects of porcelain and glass
for the exhibition
Photograph of 1945

That enemy shell of December 16 was the twenty-ninth to hit the Hermitage during the blockade. The thirtieth, which was to become the last, exploded in the Armorial Hall of the Winter Palace on January 2, 1944. It mangled the flooring, and now to be glimpsed from the Armorial Hall through the jagged hole in its floor was the rubble-strewn Rastrelli Gallery. The blast wave ripped the massive bronze chandelier out of its socket in the ceiling of the adjacent Peter the Great Hall; the magnificent parquetry artistically composed of diverse valuable woods was shattered under the impact of its crashing fall. The splinters lay in a confused mess together with the slivers of glass and the twisted bits of bronze. True, this shell did not explode fully; the unexploded part, which had wedged in the thick flooring, was extracted by army engineers and taken away.

January 26, 1944, was a day in the third winter of the Leningrad siege. Not so the morrow of January 27. The entire city was decorated with red flags and bunting, and triumphant marches poured out of the loudspeakers into homes and streets, as the announcement was broadcast: "Today

the city of Leningrad has been fully liberated from the enemy blockade." The entire country, let alone the people of Leningrad, rejoiced. The communiqué reported: "In the outcome of twelve days of fierce fighting the troops of the Leningrad Front have hurled the enemy back along the entire front, to distances of between 65 and 100 kilometres away from the city. Our forces are continuing to thrust forwards."

The special issue that the *Leningradskaya Pravda* put out to mark the lifting of the siege, was today pinned up on the notice-board in the service entrance. There had been displayed on this old notice-board for the last two and a half years running, various "orders of the day" issued by the administration and the ARP chief. Among the other things tagged up on this board had been the obituaries, wall newspapers, notices of the bread rations and announcements of the various conferences and meetings. Also displayed had been the weekly schedules of conservation work and communiqués on what had to be done urgently to repair the ravages of enemy bombing and shelling.

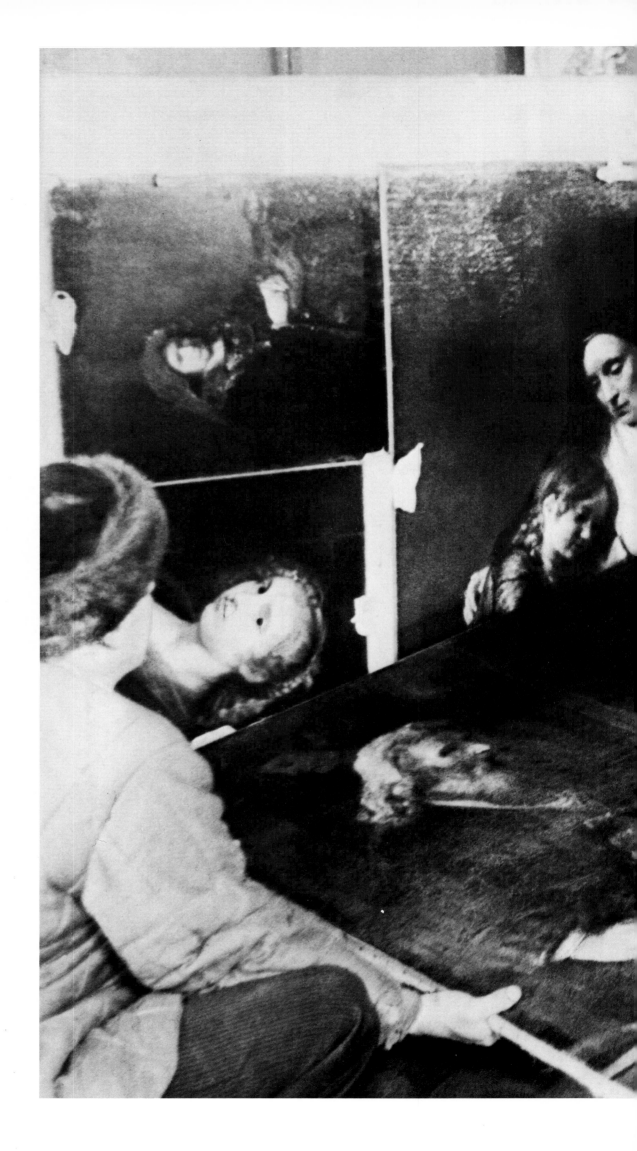

318

*The days when the paintings
were again fixed to their frames were
wonderful indeed.*

Unpacking the crates
Photograph of 1945

However, now, today, as was said before, the entire board was filled with the special issue of the *Leningradskaya Pravda*.

"Citizens of Leningrad!" begins the address of the Leningrad Front Headquarters which the Hermitage staff read in the newspaper. "Together with the fighting forces of the Leningrad Front you, courageous and staunch Leningraders, defended our beloved city from the enemy. Overcoming all the trials and tribulations of the siege by your heroic labour and iron will, you forged the sword of victory over the enemy, dedicated all your strength to the cause of victory..."

319

Caravaggio.
1571–1610. Italy
The Lute Player

319

320

321

320
Frans Hals. 1581/85–1666. Holland
Portrait of a Young Man with a Glove
in His Hand

321
Bartolomé Esteban Murillo.
1617–1682. Spain
Boy with a Dog

That evening a victory salute of twenty-four salvoes from three hundred and twenty-four guns was fired. The skies above the city lit up with bursting flares, whose multicoloured glow illumined the dark masses of the Hermitage buildings, with their mutilated walls and the empty frames of boarded-up windows unable, naturally, to reflect back the coruscating brilliance of the victory salute. However, the Hermitage stood stalwart, like a battle-scarred veteran, sharing in the honour the city had won by its defiant stand.

Though the 900-day siege was now history and the tides of war had rolled away from the city, hostilities still continued and victory was yet to be won. Martial law was still in force in Leningrad, and at the service entrance a watchwoman closely scrutinized the identity card of the news correspondent who had flown from Moscow to see how the Hermitage had weathered the blockade.

"At the door was a gray-haired elderly lady who looked more like a music teacher," wrote Tatyana Tess, a noted Soviet newspaperwoman, at the time a special correspondent for the leading Moscow-based government newspaper, *Izvestia*. She continued: "The old lady sat in a warm sheepskin and with a warm hood on her head. A rifle was propped up by her side. As she examined my identity card, a stream of bluish vapour issued from her mouth. It was so bitterly cold in there that it seemed to me as though the cold had been gathered from all over the city and had been packed and locked in this place. Right in front at the door stood as sentinels two medieval knights who had been stripped of all armour, two dummies, with no more than faded trunks on skinny legs stuffed with sawdust. By their side were crates of sand, axes, crowbars and a pair of enormous pincers."

But even before *Izvestia* came out with the story that Tatyana Tess had written, the editorial offices of various Moscow papers and the Committee for Art Affairs, let alone the Hermitage itself, had been deluged with letters, in which both soldiers at the front and factory workers and farmers in the rear wondered how the Hermitage was faring. Though many knew from the newspapers that most of its treasures had been evacuated, all wanted to know what lot had befallen the unevacuated priceless works of art and, for that matter, the magnificent architecture of the Hermitage buildings themselves. By giving prominence to the account that Tatyana Tess contributed, *Izvestia*, one of the most popular and widely read of all Soviet newspapers to this day, told its readers that the Hermitage lived on!

"The Hermitage was, and is, the country's delight. The Nazis fired their villainous heavy guns right at its heart but could not kill it." Tatyana Tess described everything seen in the battered and mauled buildings, starting with the rooms of the New Hermitage, whose glass-paned

323

324

322

Antoine Watteau. 1684–1722
France
The Capricious Girl

323

Eugène Delacroix. 1798–1863
France
Arab Saddling His Horse

324

Paul Cézanne. 1839–1906
France
The Smoker

325

326

327

325

Heinrich Imhof. 1798–1869
Germany
The Mother of Moses

326

Academician Orbeli examining
the re-evacuated statues
Photograph of 1945

327

François-Joseph Bosio. 1769–1845
France
Cupid Shooting with an Arrow

domes had been blown to smithereens in the autumn of 1941, and ending
with that hall in the Winter Palace wrecked by the last Nazi shell of January
1944, almost on the eve of Leningrad's full liberation from enemy encirclement. "Museum workers crawled all over the roof to patch up the holes; they
tied themselves by ropes to the rafters. The elderly lady who was an expert
on West European art, her heart beating wildly with fright, endlessly re-
peated: 'Like a dream. Honestly! It's like a horrible dream.' Still defying her
fear and the cutting icy wind, she climbed up the roof and nailed down the
board over the jagged hole through which the snow was seeping in."

Tatyana Tess wrote: "During the siege one needed genuine inner power
to live, not simply exist. One may definitely say of the Hermitage staff that
they lived. Today, in the quiet city that has heaved such a deep and happy

328

Bertel Thorvaldsen. 1770–1844
Denmark
Shepherd

sigh of relief, they are preparing the Hermitage's second birthday, for that near-at-hand day when real restoration work will commence. What a wonderful day that will be when the canvases return to the empty frames — it will certainly be like returning home."

The war was still being fought. However, it was receding further and further away from Leningrad where a start to heal the wounds incurred during the siege had been made. In Moscow, Iosif

Orbeli was told that very shortly the Government would require of him a detailed plan for the capital repair of all the Hermitage Museum buildings, and that in the very same year it would be necessary to commence the restoration of the main exhibition rooms and depositories. He was likewise instructed to draw up, without delay, a list of the building materials that would be needed to start restoration work.

329

The landing on the first floor of the staircase
in the New Hermitage
Photograph of 1944

Exhibition of Western European sculpture on the landing of the staircase in the New Hermitage

The list which was compiled forthwith called for sixty-five tons of gypsum plaster, eighty tons of alabaster, one hundred tons of cement, two tons of joiner's glue, forty tons of chalk plaster, thirty tons of chipped chalk, one hundred tons of asphalt mastic. (Just fancy that a few months earlier, on January 20, 1944, a mere week before the blockade had been lifted, the list of materials asked for had been of a quite different order and included: fifteen litres of kerosene oil, five (!) boxes of matches and fifteen candles.) Now the list of materials requested enumerated thirty tons of ground pigments, twenty tons of dry pigments, ten tons of white lead, twenty tons of linseed oil (but several months prior the list had included requests for merely five and a half cubic metres of plywood) and further, four thousand square

331

metres of plate glass, four thousand square metres of Bohemian glass of treble hardness, as well as double that amount of similar glass of double hardness plus two thousand metres of extra-fine glass. This was far from being all. The list of things wanted also included such items as two thousand metres of assorted canvas and thirty thousand metres of decorative fabrics, plus two tons of casting bronze, another two tons of sheet bronze, eighty kilogrammes of powdered bronze and six kilogrammes of gold leaf. Just think, the war is still going on and Soviet armed forces have yet to liberate Soviet territory of the Nazi occupying armies, but there, despite the enormous resources required not only for the fighting fronts but also for economic recovery, Orbeli was calling on the Government to provide for its restoration tons of lead and kilogrammes of gold, hundreds of cubic metres of valuable woods plus thousands of cubic metres more of coniferous woods and more and more tons of tin, wax, varnish, gelatine, nails, screws, bolts, and what not. The amounts appeared astronomical for the time, but Orbeli and his staff were sure that the Government would lavishly provide the materials required for the restoration of the Hermitage.

254

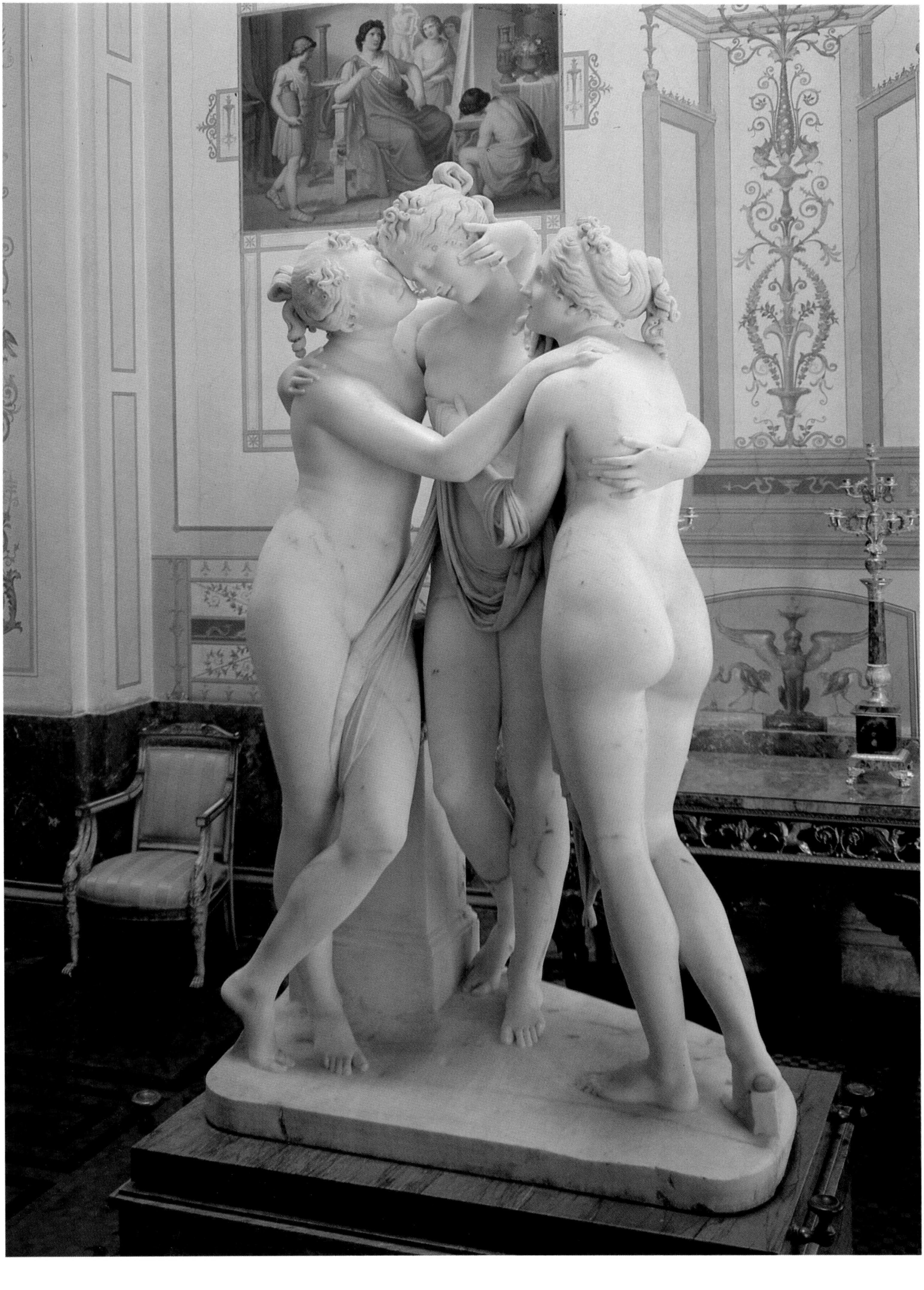

334

335

336

337

338

Though the government provision allocating the necessary resources and funds for the restoration of the Hermitage was received on August 24, 1944, it would only be fair and just to date the commencement of restoration work as that red-letter day of January 27, 1944, the day of the historic victory won at the walls of Leningrad, when the Hermitage staff first decided that, come what may, they would, in 1944, while the war was still on, arrange an exhibition of those art objects and cultural relics which had not been evacuated from the besieged city.

To achieve their purpose the Hermitage people had to have at least a few of the rooms properly repaired. They had only their own hands and skills to rely upon, as at that time, in the spring and summer of 1944, workers in the building trades, house-painters, glaziers, roofers, stucco-plasterers and the like, were not available in Leningrad. The special trades school which the municipal authorities had opened had just recruited its first batch of trainees for the professions of moulder, mason and gilder. However, the people of the Hermitage, who during the siege had put their hands to every

339

340

341

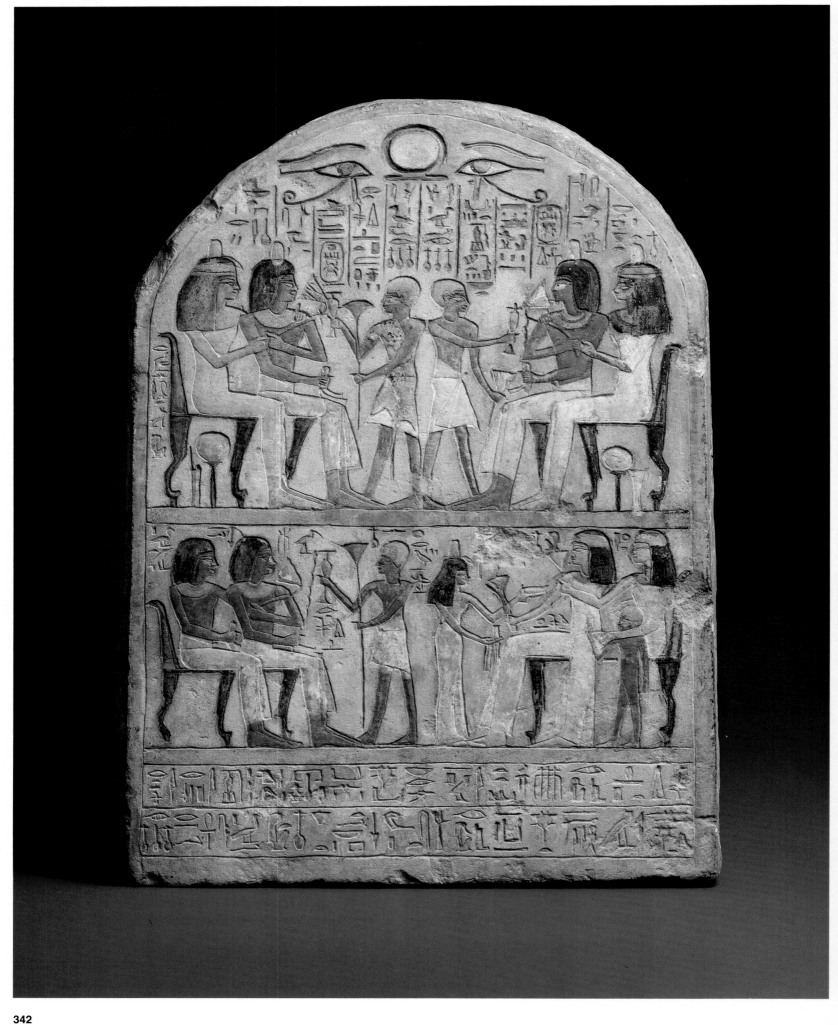

342

Tomb stone
Ancient Egypt. 15th century B.C.

conceivable kind of job, willingly set to work to prepare rooms for the exhibition on the first floor of the de La Mothe Pavilion in the Small Hermitage. Outside, they dumped the piles of sand and rubbish cluttering up the Pavilion Hall, the Gallery of Peter the Great and the Romanov Gallery and the adjacent rooms and stairs, and tidied up the parquet floors, the ceilings and the walls, even to the point of patching a hole in one wall that had been caused by an exploding shell. As a result, by autumn, both the Pavilion Hall and the Galleries were as clean as a new pin; having torn down the weather-warped plywood from the boarded-up windows, the Hermitage staff did all the glazing work needed, again with their own hands.

Now, with everything completed, the chandeliers could be re-installed. These huge cut-glass chandeliers, which three years earlier had been stowed away for safekeeping in a reliably protected cellar, had experienced much the same mishap as had overtaken the collections of porcelain deposited in the cellar beneath the Athena Hall. They, too, had been inundated,

343

Statuette of a young man
Ancient Egypt. Late 15th century B.C.

344

Statue of scribe Maaniamun
Ancient Egypt. 15th century B.C.

even though they had been slung up by ropes to trestles specially erected for the purpose. However, when the cellar was unsealed in spring, after the first blockade winter, what met the curators' eyes were chaotic jumbles of dulled bits of cut glass and green-coated bronze and tangled, rotted pieces of rope swinging from the trestles. The Hermitage researchers undertook to restore these massive lighting fixtures, and, likewise, for the first time since the start of the war, to wax and polish the parquet floors—one and a half thousand square metres(!) in the exhibition rooms.

345

French furniture in the rooms
of the Winter Palace

346

The Hermitage furniture has been returned
from evacuation
Photograph of 1945

345

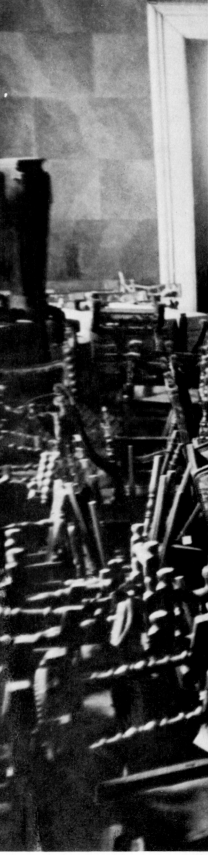

346

Restored to their pre-war sheen, the parquet floors mirrored the cut-glass clusters of twenty-eight imposing chandeliers that first glowed in full glory on November 8, 1944, the first day after the twenty-seventh anniversary of the October Revolution. As the hundreds of lights twinkled, causing the cut-glass drops to coruscate and sparkle, Orbeli clapped his hands and exclaimed with childish glee: "The chamber beamed!"

The wonderful items assembled for this very special display were representative of all of the Hermitage departments, with the exception of the bust of the Roman Emperor Marcus Aurelius, which was deliberately installed as the opening centrepiece. This bronze bust, which came to the Hermitage

in 1944, had been discovered by partisans in a ditch after they had derailed a Nazi goods train carrying metal scrap back to Germany; along with other plunder, it was to have been melted down.

"What you are going to see today in these few exhibition rooms of the Hermitage," Academician Orbeli said in his opening speech, "represents but the first step towards the full and complete restoration of the greatest museum in our country."

★   ★   ★

Leningraders always crowd Palace Square on the great national holidays. May 9, 1945, the first post-war day, was certainly no exception. The jubilant people of the Hero city packed this square to overflowing, the surplus spilling out onto the Neva's embankments. That very night the freshly washed glittering glass window panes of the Pavilion Hall of the Small Hermitage reflected the glow of the Victory Salute.

At long last the war, known in this country as the Great Patriotic War of the Soviet People, was over. The divisions and regiments that had held Leningrad and had taken Berlin were now returning home. Covered with glory, they paraded through a triumphal arch, yes, that very same triumphal arch which the architect Nikolsky had sketched during that first siege winter in Air-raid Shelter No. 3. Among the men of the Soviet Armed Forces now returning home to factory and farm were members of the Hermitage staff who had gone out to the fighting fronts. There also returned to Leningrad those people on the Hermitage staff whom evacuation had scattered throughout the distant hinterland.

Meanwhile scaffolding appeared outside and inside the Hermitage as restoration work began in earnest. Every day trucks loaded with building materials rolled through the palace gates and every

morning hundreds of artisans, practising trades that at that moment were indeed in fantastically great demand in Leningrad, entered through the Hermitage doors. Among them were not only housepainters and glaziers, not only plumbers, masons, roofers and plasterers, but also cabinet-makers, modellers, upholsterers, gilders, and workers in mosaic and marble.

On August 29, 1945, the Soviet Government issued an order to move back to the State Hermitage Museum all the collections and treasures that had been evacuated at the start of the war. A month later, Orbeli cabled Sverdlovsk that every preparation had been made to receive the collections. Immediately there came the reply that everything was ready to go, and at daybreak on October 7 two special-purpose goods trains left the Sverdlovsk goods depot, the second one an hour after the first. On October 11, Leningrad newspapers came out with the announcement that on the preceding day of October 10, all the Hermitage collections which had been evacuated to Sverdlovsk at the start of the war had arrived safely.

Now a whole convoy of trucks loaded with sealed boxes and crates slowly moved up the city's central thoroughfare of Nevsky Prospekt towards the Hermitage. Finally they reached Palace Square and the walls of the Winter Palace, which on this side were partly concealed by scaffolding; they had just been newly painted. On the embankment side, where the scaffolding had already been removed, the doors were flung wide open and there

the Hermitage curators stood, in much the same manner as four years earlier, comparing the lettering and figures stencilled on the sides of the boxes and crates being unloaded with the corresponding letters and figures in the way bills and other documents.

That boarded-up "coach," from which the marble statue of Voltaire had not "alighted" even in Sverdlovsk, was delivered straight to the entrance that the atlantes guard, and from that point was slowly windlassed up the wooden ramp which again "carpeted" all three flights of the marble staircase. Orbeli, who just a moment before had been down at the door, hurried up the stairs to welcome Voltaire back. Reassured that the statue of the philosopher was intact, he rushed along to the other end of the museum, raced down the Main Staircase, where overhead gilders were still at work, and at the entrance opening onto the Palace Embankment noted the arrival of the collection of Sassanian silver. Having accompanied the related crates on their way to the depository of the Department of the Art and Culture of the East, he hastened towards one more door, through which the treasures of the Gold Room were about to pass.

349

350

349

The Lobby
in the New Hermitage

350

*The Soviet soldiers
helped to raise the silver
Tomb of Alexander Nevsky,
Russian Grand Duke
and military commander
of the thirteenth century.*

Photograph of 1945

351

*Fifteen thousand kilogrammes
of silver were used by
St Petersburg masters
for making the Tomb.*

The Tomb of Alexander
Nevsky
Russia. 1747–52

353

353
Goblets of coloured glass painted in gold
Russia, St Petersburg.
Second half of the 18th century

354
Russian glassware painted in enamels
St Petersburg.
First half of the 19th century

354

355

352, 355

*The hall where the Alexander
Nevsky Tomb stands displays
Russian glass.*

The Concert Hall in the Winter
Palace
Designed by Bartolommeo
Francesco Rastrelli, 1753–59;
rebuilt by Vasily Stasov, 1837–39

"Unloading commenced at 8:30 a.m. on October 11 and finished at 1 p.m. on October 13," Orbeli reported to the Chairman of the State Committee for Art Affairs in Moscow. "There were no break-downs or any other unfortunate occurrences either during unloading at the goods depot, or en route, or during unloading at the Hermitage. Verification of the crates delivered established full and complete identity of the crates and boxes as numbered and lettered when evacuated in 1941 aboard the first and second special-purpose trains. Hanging of pictures commenced on November 14."

What wonderful days those were when the canvases were re-installed in their frames. Now back again in their old frames were Rembrandt's *Portrait of an Old Man in Red*, *Portrait of a Young Man with a Lace Collar*, *The Holy Family*, *Danaë*, *Flora* and *The Return of the Prodigal Son*. The scholar from Amsterdam again looked down from his gilt carved mounting. He seemed to have lifted his eyes from the manuscript lying before him and be intently watching the restorers unwinding that roller around which ten priceless canvases had been rolled, among them *Abraham's Sacrifice* and *The Descent from the Cross*.

As more crates were carried in and deposited on the floor of the sixty-eight rooms that had been repaired and tidied specially to accept the re-evacuated treasures, curators could again be seen bending over them, as they had done when packing the Hermitage Museum collections for evacuation. And once again piles of shavings, clumps of cotton wool, wrinkled paper and oilcloth were strewn around in confusion.

The paintings, the statues, the porcelain, the majolica, the glassware, the antique vases and the Scythian gold objects were all to go back where they had stood, hung or lain before, in full conformity with their pre-war locations. True, years later, when all the restoration work was fully and finally completed and a total of three hundred and forty-five rooms were opened for display, much would change in those rooms that had been made the venue for the Hermitage's first post-war exhibition — so necessary to reassure Leningrad's art lovers that everything would be as it had been before.

There were only a few days to go before the celebration of the twenty-eighth anniversary of the October Revolution. Leningrad had already been decorated with red bunting for the festive event. Indeed, on the morning of November 4, it seemed to the Hermitage Museum staff hurrying along the Palace Embankment to the service entrance that the place had been bedecked specially to mark their museum's great day.

The elderly ladies, the little old ladies serving as room attendants, took their places in the gilt plush chairs on the different floors. By that Sunday morning of November 4, 1945, sixty-eight of the Hermitage rooms and halls shone in all the splendour that had been theirs on that fateful Sunday morning of June 22, 1941, the day the Nazi invasion began.

Meanwhile the guests invited for this very special opening gathered on all flights of the ceremonial staircase of the New Hermitage. More and more visitors poured in through the doors at which the granite atlantes stood sentinel. (The Main Entrance on the Palace Embankment side was re-opened three weeks later, on November 25.) There had come for this festive occasion many of those art workers who at the start of the war had helped the Hermitage staff to pack the collections for evacuation; there had come the demobbed officers and men of the victorious Soviet Armed Forces; there had come factory workers and engineers and those building workers who had restored the war-ravaged edifices of the museum to their pristine glory; there had come the professors and students of Leningrad University, Academy of Arts and Conservatoire. Present as guests of honour were representatives of the local and central committees of the Soviet Communist Party and the Soviet Government, whose thoughtful solicitude the Hermitage staff had always felt, both during the war and in times of peace. They were welcomed by the Hermitage staff, by those who had stood guard over the museum throughout the ordeal of the 900-day siege and by those who had kept safe the priceless collections evacuated far to the rear.

As Academician Iosif Orbeli raised his hand a deep hush descended. His address to the guests was brief, very brief, as he so eagerly and impatiently desired to utter the short phrase: "The Hermitage is open!"

356 Nuremberg. The International Military Tribunal in session
(Iosif Orbeli in the witness-box)

Academician Orbeli: "The Nazi shelling of the Hermitage was deliberate; this was absolutely clear to both myself and my entire staff for the simple reason that it was methodical, not random, haphazard, the same as the bombardment to which the entire city was subjected for months on end."

357 Major Nazi war criminals are being tried in Nuremberg

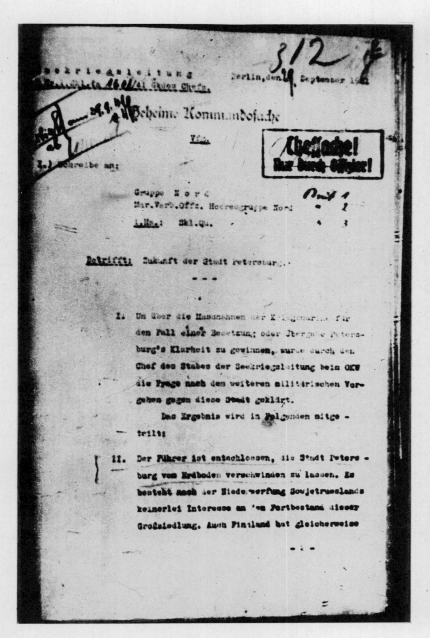
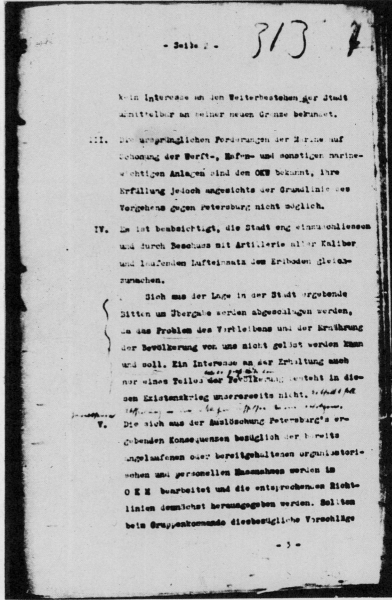

358 The Directive of the Nazi Command of September 29, 1941,
referring to Hitler's decision to destroy Leningrad.
This document was presented by the American prosecution
at the Nuremberg Trial

...*Hitler has decided to wipe St. Petersburg
off the map.*

*...It is proposed to establish a tight blockade of
the city and, by shelling it with artillery of all calibres
and incessant bombing by the air force, level it to
the ground.*

*If conditions in the city should reach a point that
would bring offers of surrender, such offers should
be rejected, inasmuch as the solution of the problems
of preserving and feeding the population is neither
possible nor our duty. For our part, in this war that is
a matter of life and death, we are not interested
in the survival of even a fraction of the population
of so large a city.*

★   ★   ★

We are again back in Nuremberg where the International Military Tribunal is trying major Nazi war criminals. Academician Orbeli is at the witness-box.

"Do you possess any knowledge as to the destruction of art objects and cultural monuments in Leningrad?" the Soviet prosecutor asks.

"Yes, I do possess such knowledge."

"Could you please present this High Court with all the facts you are in possession of?"

"The venerable academician spoke as if quoting an indictment," newspapers reported — although all that he presented were bare facts, facts that could not be denied. He cited the number of shells that Nazi gunners had fired at the Hermitage. He cited the number of bombs that Nazi airmen had dropped on it. He spoke of the shell that had scarred the granite atlantes and of the shells that had exploded within the Hermitage. He then enumerated the architectural monuments of Leningrad that had been wrecked by Nazi bombardment and described the ruins he personally had witnessed in suburban Peterhof, Pushkin and Pavlovsk. He then again spoke of the Hermitage. "The Nazi shelling of the Hermitage was deliberate; this was absolutely clear to both myself and my entire staff," he said, "for the simple reason that it was methodical, not random, haphazard, the same as the bombardment to which the entire city was subjected for months on end."

In an attempt to confute his evidence, the counsel for the defence argued the point. The lawyer defending the Hitlerite General Staff asked: "How competent is the witness in artillery matters to say that the shelling was deliberate?"

Academician Iosif Orbeli replied with quiet dignity: "True enough, I have never been a gunner. But I will say that while thirty shells hit the Hermitage, only one hit the nearby bridge, which allows me to state with complete conviction as to what the Nazis were aiming at. As far as that is concerned I am gunner enough!"

"When drafting their insensate schemes to achieve world supremacy," the Soviet prosecutor declared at the Nuremberg trial, "the Hitlerite plotters planned a crusade against world culture besides unleashing wars of pillage and plunder. They sought to turn the clock of civilization back. Arrogantly encroaching upon humanity's future, they trampled the finest heritage of humanity's past. In the unprecedented combat between culture and obscurantism, between civilization and barbarity, it was culture and civilization that emerged victorious."

359

The Small Hermitage
Designed by Jean-Baptiste Vallin de La Mothe.
1767–69

ГОСУДАРСТВЕННЫЙ
ЭРМИТАЖ
ВНОВЬ ОТКРЫТЫ
ДЛЯ ОБОЗРЕНИЯ ЗАЛЫ

ИТАЛЬЯНСКОЙ ЖИВОПИСИ XVII—XVIII веков

ИСПАНСКОЙ ЖИВОПИСИ XVII—XVIII веков

ФЛАМАНДСКОЙ ЖИВОПИСИ и ГРАФИКИ

ФРАНЦУЗСКОГО ПРИКЛАДНОГО ИСКУССТВА XVII—XVIII веков

ЗАЛ ФАРФОРА XVIII века

**Музей открыт ежедневно, кроме понедельников,
с 11 до 18 часов**

Выставки искусства Франции XVIII века и французского прикладного
искусства открыты по вторникам и четвергам, выставка западно-
европейского искусства XIX века — по средам и пятницам

Вход о Дворцовой набережной, Главный подъезд

Все справки и записи на экскурсии в Отделе Просветработы Государственного Эрмитажа,
Дворцовая Набережная, 36, с 10 до 18 часов. Телефон 4-71-10

БИ 1137 УЛ—4 Зак. 2265 Тир. 500. 10.VI.46 г.

360

*As the Main
Entrance to the
Winter Palace was
still under restoration,
the visitors invited to
attend the re-opening
ceremony were
ascending the Main
Staircase in the New
Hermitage.*

The Main Staircase
in the New Hermitage
Built by Vasily Stasov
and Nikolai Yefimov
after Leo von
Klenze's design.
1842–51

361

The poster reads:
"The Hermitage
rooms are again
open for the public..."

362

The Greater
Skylighted Room
in the New Hermitage

363

Giovanni Battista Tiepolo. 1696–1770. Italy
Maecenas Presenting the Liberal Arts to Augustus

Giorgione. 1478–1510. Italy
Judith

365

Albrecht Dürer. 1471–1528. Germany
Allegory of Justice

366

Pierre Dumoustier. After 1540 – after 1600. France
Portrait of Etienne Dumoustier

fait le xi de
juin 1569

367

Lucas Cranach the Elder. 1472–1553. Germany
The Virgin and Child under the Apple-tree

368

Caspar David Friedrich. 1774–1840. Germany
On a Sailing Ship

369

Anthony van Dyck. 1599–1641. Flanders
Self-portrait

371

Peter Paul Rubens. 1577–1640. Flanders
Bacchus

372

Peter Paul Rubens. 1577–1640. Flanders
Portrait of a Lady-in-Waiting to the Infanta Isabella

373
Etienne-Maurice Falconet. 1716–1791. France
Flora

374
Auguste Rodin. 1840–1917. France
Eternal Spring

375

376

378

375

Russian stone carvings.
19th century

376

Objects of malachite and glass
Russia. 19th century

377

Objects of silver
Russia, Tula. 19th century

378

The Fabergé pieces
St Petersburg.
Late 19th – early 20th centuries

379

Spanish glass
Andalusia. 16th–18th centuries

380

Venetian glass. Late 19th century

381

Venetian glass. 16th–17th centuries

380

381

379

383

382
Saucepan and ewer
Byzantium. 6th century

383
The mosaic icon of St Theodore
Byzantium. Early 14th century

384
Diptych with circus scenes
Byzantium. 6th century

385

Terra-cotta statuettes from Tanagra. 4th–3rd centuries B.C.

386

Hercules and the Lion
Roman copy after an original by Lysippus
of the 4th century B.C.

387

The Hercules Room in the New Hermitage
Built by Vasily Stasov and Nikolai Yefimov
after Leo von Klenze's design. 1842–51

388

*The Hermitage, which was saved for humanity
during the Second World War, is one of the
most famous museums in the world.*

ПОДВИГ ЭРМИТАЖА

БЛОКАДА ЛЕНИНГРАДА. 1941–1944

ИЗДАТЕЛЬСТВО „АВРОРА". ЛЕНИНГРАД. 1985

Изд. № 1296

Printed and bound in Finland